Folktales of the Amazon

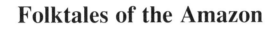

"In backyards dolphins strum their guitars, charming the girls."

Folktales of the Amazon

Juan Carlos Galeano

Translated by Rebecca Morgan and Kenneth Watson
Foreword by Michael Uzendoski

LIBRARIES
UNLIMITED
A Member of the Greenwood Publishing Group
Westport, Connecticut • London

Library of Congress Cataloging-in-Publication Data
Galeano, Juan Carlos, 1958–
Folktales of the Amazon / Juan Carlos Galeano; translated by Rebecca Morgan and Kenneth
Watson; foreword by Michael Uzendoski.
   p. cm.
  Includes bibliographical references and index.
  ISBN 978-1-59158-674-6 (alk. paper)
  1. Indians of South America—Amazon River Region—Folklore. 2. Tales—Amazon River
Region. 3. Amazon River Region—Folklore. I. Title.
F2519.1.A6G35 2009
398.20981′1—dc22   2008028653

British Library Cataloguing in Publication Data is available.

Library of Congress Catalog Card Number: 2008028653
ISBN: 978-1-59158-674-6

First published in 2009

Libraries Unlimited, 88 Post Road West, Westport, CT 06881
A Member of the Greenwood Publishing Group, Inc.
www.lu.com

Printed in the United States of America

The paper used in this book complies with the
Permanent Paper Standard issued by the National
Information Standards Organization (Z39.48–1984).

10 9 8 7 6 5 4 3 2 1

Epigraph (page ii) from "Leticia" (Leticia) by Juan Carlos Galeano. Translated by James Kimbrell
and Rebecca Morgan. *Indiana Review*, vol. 28 (Summer 2006): 90–93.
Watercolor drawings and appendix illustrations created by Jaime Luis Choclote. Used with
permission.
Story illustration created by Juana Hianaly Galeano. Used with permission.
Map of the Amazon provided by Richie Kent. Used with permission.

to Noemí Eleanor

TABLE OF CONTENTS

Foreword ix
Acknowledgments xiii
Introduction. xv
  The Amazon. xvi
  Map. xvii
  How the Amazonian Tales in This Book Came to Be xviii
  The Tales. xxi
  Intended Audience and Use for This Book xxv

Chapter 1: Tales of Origin

Moniyamena: The Origin of the Amazon River 3
Vitória Régia: Giant Water Lily 5

Chapter 2: Tales about Anacondas and Boas

Huayramama: Snake Mother of the Wind 9
Sachamama: Mother of the Forest 11
Yakumama: Mother of All Water Beings 13
Juan Boa: The Man Who Turned into a River Serpent 15

Chapter 3: Tales about Dolphins and Other Aquatic Seducers

María and the Dolphins 19
The Girl and the Anaconda. 21
A Gift from Yara, an Underwater Seducer 23
Yakuruna: Male Lover from the Underwater World 25
The City of the Dolphins. 27
Mawaris: Aquatic Abductors. 30
Yara: Fish-Woman from the Underwater World. 32
The Dolphin's Children. 34

Chapter 4: Tales of Beasts and Forest Defenders

Mapinguari: One-Eyed Ogre 39
Curupira: Guardian Spirit of the Forest 41

Chullachaki: Owner of Trees and Animals 43
Amasanga Warmi: A Ferocious Wife 45
Epereji: Animal Guardian 47
Curupira's Son 49
Seringa: Mother of the Rubber Trees 51
The Flute of the Chullachaki 53
The Hunter and the Curupira 56
Yanapuma: Black Jaguar Vampire 58

Chapter 5: Tales of Dark and Malevolent Shamans

Kanaima: Dark Shamans 63
The Spirits of the Stones: Evil Spirits 66
Pact with the Devil 69
Dañero: Malicious Sorcerer 71
Matinta-Perera: Devious People Turn into Birds 73
Pusanga: Love Ointment 75

Chapter 6: Tales of Punishment for Ill Behavior

Lamparilla: Glowing Ghost 81
Runamula: Women of Ill Repute Turn into Mules 83
Cowboy Quemdera 85
Caballococha: A Town Plagued by Ill Behavior 87

Chapter 7: Tales of Special Places, Plants, and Birds

The Enchanted City 91
Renacal: A Grove of Magical Trees 93
Boa Plants: Plants Turn into Animals 95
Ayaymama: A Bird Who Cries Like a Human 97
Lupuna: A Tree Becomes Vengeful 99
Chicua: Messenger Bird 101
Pumayuyu: A Plant with Magical Powers 103

Glossary of Vernacular and Scientific Names 105
Bibliography 109
Appendix: Animals and Plants of Amazonian Cuisine 113
Index 123

FOREWORD

"It would seem that mythological worlds have been built up only to be shattered again, and that new worlds were built from the fragments."

(Franz Boas, 1898)

Juan Carlos Galeano, a poet and translator, grew up in the area of the Caquetá River of the Colombian Amazon. However, like many of us, he made his life far away from his natal home and did not think it a place of much interest. While living abroad, Galeano came to see Amazonia in a different light and as a source of poetic and literary inspiration. He had a change of heart and decided to embark on a project to record and study folktales from places throughout the region—Peru, Colombia, Ecuador, Venezuela, Bolivia, Brazil, and British Guyana.

The author taped the stories and, while listening to them, reworked them and wrote them down. He used his poetic sensibilities to draft them in a way that was faithful to their spirit but different from their original form. This is a rather unique way of doing an oral literature or folklore project. The folklorist tries to stay faithful to what is "on the tape," perhaps presenting the story in the original language with a translation of the word-by-word transcription. A linguist might add special terminology to point out the grammatical features of speech involved, or someone trained in ethnopoetics would divide the story into acts, scenes, stanzas, verses, and lines. What often happens in such a process is that the art of the oral narrative and the experience of listening to it becomes lost, since the story has been subjected to the conventions of social scientific or linguistic discourse.

Galeano has offered us another option that derives from how storytellers and poets, rather than social scientists, do things. Storytellers are mostly concerned with telling a good story, and they innovate constantly to reflect both their circumstances and audiences. He has gone to great pains to make these stories readable and aesthetically pleasing while also remaining faithful to the spirit of the mythology that defines them. He has found a way to write down oral literature to convey something of the experience of listening to a tale *en vivo* (live). I can hear the stories as I read them, a feeling I do not get when reading stories done via the genre of social scientific analysis. The lyrical quality of Galeano's writing comes through, but, more than a poet, He engages in a technique of shamanism that he learned from his experiences deep in the Amazon.

Research among shamans in Amazonia shows that sensory crossing-over, or synesthesia, is a core method of how shamans and patients feel the presence of the divine powers and spirits through aesthetic experiences. For example, reflecting on his work with healers in Putumayo (see Taussig 1987), Taussig considers how non-visual senses work mimetically and cross over with vision to create powerful physical reactions (such as nausea, which he experiences working with medicines in Putumayo): "the senses cross over and translate into each other. You feel redness. You see music ... seeing is felt in a nonvisual way. You move into the interior of images, just as images move into you" (Taussig 1993: 57–58). Galeano here has mastered this trick. He is like the shaman, and the reader the patient; the author transports us into a new mimetic reality through his art. The beauty of the folktales, masterfully translated by Rebecca Ann Morgan and Kenneth Watson, allow the English reader to experience these stories as if they were not translated at all. One feels and hears the power of the Amazonian world through a foreign language. It is like dreaming and reading at the same time.

Two further ideas need to be explored for the reader to appreciate these tales. The first is the "perspectivist" nature of Amazonian cosmologies; the second is the rather fluid boundary between mestizo and indigenous cultures throughout Amazonia.

Amazonian cultures have been shown to abide by a complex philosophy termed "perspectivism," the notion that "the world is inhabited by different sorts of subjects or persons, human and non-human, which apprehend reality from distinct points of view" (Viveiros de Castro 1998: 469; Uzendoski, Hertica, and Calapucha 2005; Uzendoski 2005; Vilaça 2002). In telling the story of a mythical event, for example, various perspectives are entailed and their depiction is integral to the art, but the common humanity of all living beings is emphasized. The complexity of this worldview derives from the fact that animals consider themselves as humans and that it is the ontological divide of the levels of the world that makes people see animals as animals. There are moments when the boundary between this world and other worlds cracks, and people can see animals in their true human form. When such corridors do open, there are moments of danger and power.

A common theme of this boundary-crossing involves sexuality and sexual relations—anacondas and dolphins, it would seem, are not only "good to think" as Claude Lévi-Strauss would say, but they are also "good to sleep with." People are sometimes taken to the underworld by their animal lovers and end up living with them in great cities, never to return. They have children and live among family. At other times, animals from below appear in this world and are adopted and raised by human parents. The defining concepts are kinship and a common humanity between people and animals, spirits, and other forest beings.

Transformation and shape-shifting, rather than fixity, are the basic premises of Amazonian existence. What the mythology as a whole conveys is how the world came to be through a series of transformations—often violent and predatory—in which the current boundaries became established. These boundaries, however, can and often are crossed by shamans and others through experiences like dreams, storytelling, humor, illness, tragedy, and ritual ceremonies. Galeano's book conveys the complexity and richness of this boundary-crossing. He also shows that there is such a thing as an Amazonian

Foreword

aesthetic of the world, one that is still living and perhaps thriving—in spite of what modernist discourses may say—among mestizo peoples as well as the indigenous. Shamanic experience is alive and well in the Amazonian world. Even if one is not a shaman, people still experience shamanic realities through stories and other means.

The last topic is one of cultural and ethnic boundaries. These stories, while told by mestizo people in Spanish, derive from the indigenous world. Much recent research has shown that the boundary between mestizo and indigenous is more fluid than previously thought; this book reveals this fluidity. Stories travel, but so too do the cosmologies represented within them. Underlying this book is the sense that modernity is not simply replacing indigenous realities (in a linear fashion) with rationalistic truths about the world. Amazonian realities are still a present and active part of the lives of the non-indigenous, who now represent the majority of the population in most cities throughout the region. I have described these relations elsewhere as an "alternative modernity," a concept that can be defined as, "sites of creative adaptation by which people are questioning the present by way of cultural knowledge (Gaonkar 2001: 1–23). The indigenous are the background interlocutors of these stories, but they are also a defining part of the present dynamic by which modernity is transformed. In the story "A Gift from Yara, an Underwater Seducer," for example, an indigenous man takes on the role of shamanic interpreter and explains what happened when a man from Lima has a troubling experience with a fish-woman. The man from Lima also possesses a dolphin tooth given to him by an indigenous friend. One can imagine such encounters and interactions throughout Amazonia, where people from the outside are actively taught by natives to see the world, and their experiences, from their perspective.

Indeed, anthropologists are now rethinking the concept of boundaries altogether. I especially like an article by Ira Bashkow (2004) in this regard, who uses neo-Boasian ideas about diffusion and linguistic notions of the "isogloss" (a dialect boundary) to argue for a more nuanced sense of boundaries as sites of "differentiation" but which do not, by themselves, exclude or contain (Bashkow 2004: 450). The boundaries between various cultures in Amazonia are there—I am not suggesting they are not—but their presence invites flow and boundary crossing, a process much like the complex linguistic overlap/differentiation that occurs among dialects of a language. Bashkow (2004: 451), for example, writes that, "contrary to our naive view of dialects as discrete entities, the isoglosses of distinct features often fail to coincide; instead they form tangled patterns of crisscrosses and loops, making it impossible to establish a definitive line of demarcation between dialects." I think this is the case with these stories. They represent a "tangled pattern" of crisscrossing and looping with coterminous indigenous and mestizo worlds.

The perspectivism reflected in the stories herein reflects an Amazonian theorization of this problem in which boundary crossing and "looping" are major themes. The storytellers are less concerned with cultural boundaries than they are with natural ones, but all "boundaries are meant to be crossed" in the Amazonian world, to borrow a phrase from Santos-Granero (2002). This discussion leads me to my final point, which is that these stories contain principles and ideas that are relevant to our own lives. These stories allow readers to see other cultures as part of a greater intercultural world, and also invite readers to see themselves as part of a greater internatural world as well. People and human reproduction are intimately connected to the environment, which, although not seen as such in normal reality, reflects a deeper and underlying common humanity shared by all living things. These are salient insights relevant to today's world, where boundaries have now become barriers and nature merely an object to be exploited for economic gain rather than human progress. The current trend is one of the impoverishment of our connectivity to others and to our world, a set of relations Karl Marx described as alienation and which is still with us in different historical form (see Gregory 1997). I think it is a great achievement that Galeano has conveyed the deep wisdom and complexity of Amazonian thought through an English-language book. Most of us who are native speakers of English must spend years or decades in Amazonia to see and comprehend such relations. I hope that Galeano's gift will help others to better appreciate the beauty and complexity of the human condition as seen from an Amazonian perspective.

Michael Uzendoski
Florida State University

References

Bashkow, Ira. "A Neo-Boasian Conception of Cultural Boundaries." *American Anthropologist*, vol. 106, no. 3 (September 2004): 443–458.

Gaonkar, Dilip Parameshwar, ed. *Alternative Modernities*. Durham, NC: Duke University Press, 2001.

Gregory, Christopher. *The Savage Money: The Anthropology and Politics of Commodity Exchange*. Amsterdam: Harwood Academic Publishers, 1997.

Santos-Granero, Fernando. "Boundaries are Meant to be Crossed: The Magic and Politics of the Long-lasting Amazon/Andes Divide." *Identities: Global Studies in Culture and Power* 9(4) (2002): 545–569.

Taussig, Michael. *Mimesis and Alterity: A Particular History of the Senses*. New York: Routlege, 1993.

———. *Shamanism, Colonialism, and the Wild Man: A Study in Terror and Healing*. Chicago: University of Chicago Press, 1987.

Uzendoski, Michael. "Making Amazonia: Shape-Shifters, Giants, and Alternative Modernities." *Latin American Research Review* 40(1) (2004): 223–236 (book review essay).

———. *The Napo Runa of Amazonian Ecuador*. Interpretations of Culture in the New Millennium Series. Urbana and Chicago: University of Illinois Press, 2005.

Uzendoski, Michael, Hertica, Mark, and Calapucha, Edith. "Making Kin Out of Others in Amazonia." *Journal of the Royal Anthropological Institute (N.S.)* 8 (2002): 347–365.

———. "The Phenomenology of Perspectivism: Aesthetics, Sound, and Power, in Napo Runa Women's Songs of Upper Amazonia." *Current Anthropology* 46(4) (2005): 656–662 (peer reviewed).

———. Vilaça, Aparecida, "Making Kin Out of Others in Amazonia." Journal of the Royal anthropological Institute (N.S.) 8 (2002): 347–365.

Viveiros de Castro, Eduardo. "Cosmological Deixis and Amerindian Perspectivism." *Journal of the Royal Anthropological Institute* 41, no. 4 (1998): 469–488.

ACKNOWLEDGMENTS

I am grateful to the many people who helped me in the research and production of this book. I want to recognize the financial support I had from Florida State University in the form of a summer grant to begin research on this project in the summer of 1996, my first trip back to the basin since I left the Colombian Amazon in the early 1980s. I would also like to express thanks to the Winthrop-King Institute and the Department of Modern Languages and Linguistics at Florida State University for the financial assistance they provided on several occasions over the additional ten years of fieldwork I spent conducting research in the Amazonian arcas of Brazil, Bolivia, Colombia, Ecuador, Guyana, Perú, and Venezuela.

I am very grateful to Libraries Unlimited senior editor Barbara Ittner, whose patience and help has been instrumental in the preparation of the manuscript. I am thankful for assistance from Chuck McCann, director of Florida State University's Strozier Library Digital Media Center, and W. Malcolm Shackelford, FSU library associate, who offered technical assistance in preparing the book's graphics. I would like to thank Rebecca Morgan and Ken Watson for undertaking the English translation of these folktales. Amazonian painter Jaime Luis Choclote and geographer Richie Kent helped contextualize the stories by providing illustrations and familiarizing readers with the geography of the region.

I owe gratitude to anthropologist Michael Uzendoski, my colleague and friend, for inspiring conversations about the Amazonian way of thinking. I also would like to thank geographer and friend Nigel J. H. Smith for his comments on the first version of this collection. I am grateful to biologist Elsa Rengifo at the Institute for Research in the Peruvian Amazon (IIAP) in Iquitos, Peru, for her guidance on medicinal plants and to Peruvian anthropologist Alberto Chirif for reading and commenting on the Spanish version of the manuscript. Any errors or mistakes in this book are my responsibility.

Most of all I want to thank the storytellers and friends who live in the rivers, forests, and small settlements throughout Amazonia. It would be impossible to name and to express my gratitude to the people in the many places throughout the basin who opened their hearts and hosted me in their homes. Along with the tales they told me, they confided in me their views of the world, something that helped me immensely in recasting their stories.

I would like these tales to be a homage to the people, plants, animals, and spirits of the Amazon.

INTRODUCTION

The Amazon

In 1542, expeditionist friar Gaspar de Carvajal recorded the way he and his shipmates reacted with fascination to native tales about fierce Amazonian women and the riches and wealth awaiting them downstream on their journeys. Today, there are still plentiful accounts of the Amazon, including tales that paint it as a land of wonder and beauty and stories that tell of its destruction and devastation. These accounts include reports from French explorer Jacques-Yves Cousteau, magazine articles, television shows, travel logs, biological and environmental data, and advocacy for indigenous rights by media personalities such as the rock star Sting. Such varying approaches continue to build on our complex perception of Amazonia and lead to the fascination that the inhabitants of the rest of the Earth have with the Amazon. A vast territory almost the size of the continental United States, Amazonia is the habitat of the greatest number of plants and animals in the world. Situated in the equatorial region of the planet, the Amazon is a territory shared by Brazil, Colombia, Ecuador, Peru, Bolivia, Venezuela, and Guyana.

Over the last 500 years, this exuberance of fragile green earth, which has been inhabited for between 40,000 and 60,000 years, has received a parade of conquistadors, travelers, and adventurers seeking riches, as well as immigrants in search of a new home. They have brought with them domesticated animals, tools for working the land, religious traditions, and Western mythologies full of fantastic creatures symbolic of their beliefs. Newcomers came into contact with native inhabitants who practiced slash-and-burn farming in small segments of the forest to produce sufficient food, collected fruits from the trees, and obtained protein through hunting and fishing.

More than 800 indigenous ethnic groups, speaking languages predominantly of the Arawak, Carib, and Tupian families, once lived in this region. They had more than enough to feed themselves, thanks to practices that permitted them to produce food or to obtain animals from the forest without causing major changes to the environment. Their cosmological systems or worldviews about origins, the future, and their place in the universe provided them with their religiosity and explanations about their existence. This belief system also supplied regulations and codes of behavior. Amazonians regarded the rain forest as a world of spirits, animals, souls, and humans whose intermingling of substance or energy binds them together. At night, the natives gathered in huts and around fires to listen to stories told by their elders, who spoke of the world's creation through acts of love, violence, predations, and constant interactions between the natural and supernatural world. Their tales spoke of their adventures and daily negotiations with the fantastic. There, powerful and whimsical creatures, mythical snakes, ogres, defenders of the forests, beautiful females, and handsome males capable of transformation walked the pathways and populated the rivers creating a sense of awe, and also fear. The mythological creatures in their dreams and stories advised adult community members on places for hunting or fishing and warned them about rules of behavior while engaging in these activities, showing them an ecological way to live in the world.

Newcomers brought their traditions and histories along with different ideas about interacting with nature, animals, and trees. Outsiders from distant, modern cities related to the forest by sending orders for medicines or fine materials to improve their quality of life, make them rich, or bring progress to their cities. Since colonial times, indigenous inhabitants, *mestizos* (people of mixed blood of European and Amerindians), and descendants of African slaves have produced cocoa beans, Brazilian nuts, medicinal plants, lumber, animal hides, rubber, and, more recently, petroleum, gold, cocaine, and other products for export.

At the turn of the twentieth century, the growing need for rubber in the Western world escalated. The bicycle craze began in 1890 in Europe, and later the demand for tires for the first Western cars increased the need for Amazonian rubber. A desire for wealth, embellished by tales about fortunes made by a few entrepreneurs through the extraction of rubber, created a fever for the "white gold" of the Amazon, much like the gold rush in California. This led people from Europe, the United States, and many Amazonians into the forest to tap rubber trees in the wild. The existence of fine wood for furniture in this rich terrestrial ecosystem also attracted the attention of Westerners and led to the harvesting of cedar, mahogany, and many other species of trees. Sales of heron feathers and alligator, jaguar, and manatee skins for the fabrication of shoes and other goods to be sold in the finest shops initiated new hunting practices and transformed the way of life for many indigenous people.

Now, at the turn of the twenty-first century, Amazonian forests and rivers have experienced unprecedented population growth and deforestation as cattle farming and large-scale cultivation increase and encroach. Extraction of timber, drilling for oil in the forest, and the search for minerals such as bauxite and gold have given employment to the local population, but have also had negative effects, devastating in some places, on the biological richness, as well as having a drastic impact on the lives of the indigenous groups and the cultural traditions of Amazonians. The results of systematic destruction of land containing such a vast diversity of life threaten humans who live far from the rain forest and have brought international attention to Amazonia.

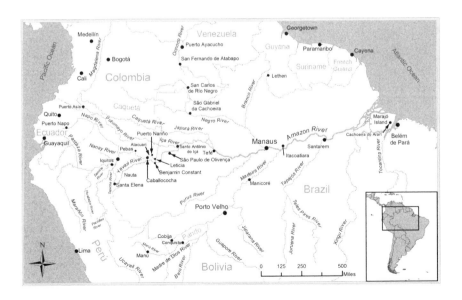

How the Amazonian Tales in This Book Came to Be

In the area of the Caquetá or Yapurá River, one of the biggest tributaries of the Amazon, I lived on a small farm with my grandparents, a couple of miles from the settlement where I went to elementary school. In those days, I liked to hear stories about the spirits of the forest and underwater world that the native people who helped my grandfather would tell at the dinner table. I always listened and asked them to tell more, though as the evening grew late, I would pay a high price, for I couldn't sleep afterward. I thought the spirits would come get me for asking too much about them.

In 1983, I left Colombia, but I didn't forget the tales I had heard. After spending years abroad, I decided to investigate the stories told by people in different parts of the Amazon. In 1996, I traveled to the region to collect more stories, or story fragments, and recast them. I was inspired to do this because I was not content with the written versions of Amazonian folktales I had read. I was displeased with the way stories had been recreated or retold, warped from their local oral traditions and often describing the indigenous inhabitants as savages and classifying the forest within the dichotomy of heaven or hell. I didn't like the excessive flowery and ornate language used by the Amazonian writers who had retold the folktales, heavily influenced by the traits of so-called French Parnasianism (the artistic mode of poetic writing adopted by Latin American writers at the turn of the twentieth century). Furthermore, existing collections of folktales were specific to only one area of a single country. There were numerous illuminating studies of native folktales done by linguists and anthropologists, but they were critical studies specific to those fields.

Since my literary work has been in poetry, the project was not only a trip to the past but also a writer's challenge. I imagined that some of these tales from my past were still available. My quest started in Leticia, a Colombian port on the Amazon River at the border of Peru and Brazil. The night I arrived, I began to search for the folktales. I met Manuel Sangama in one of the floating restaurants. He told me his mother knew a lot of stories.

The next day after playing soccer with his brothers in front of the house, we ate dinner and Manuel's mother told us about spirits of the jungle and pink dolphins. "These *bujeos*," she said, employing the word used for dolphins that I heard from Uitoto descendants in my childhood in Caquetá, "would come out at night in the form of handsome fair-skinned young men to charm girls."

From then on, my search for folktales took me to other places in the Amazon basin. In Brazilian towns along the Amazon and Yavari rivers, I learned about the *Mapinguari*. This animal protector is a hairy beast with one eye, a feature introduced most likely by Europeans out of Greek mythology. According to María Bezerra, a woman who made her living by running a food stand for boatmen, passengers, street vendors, and the longshoremen unloading lumber boats, the Mapingauri is very dangerous to stubborn hunters. I heard more stories about the Mapinguari while staying in the hut of Don Luis Da Silva, an old hunter who hadn't been out lately because of new regulations and advancing blindness.

Traveling on long trips in the Amazon and its tributaries offered me an opportunity to find out about the different guardian spirits, medicinal properties of plants, and lore about the river. On a five-day trip upstream in a big cargo boat on my way to Iquitos, I had the opportunity to hear stories from one of the crewmembers about the *Yakumama*, a supernatural snake able to produce big waves and hold the boat on her body for a few minutes. Other members of the crew swore to the veracity of the tale.

Two years later, I heard a similar story about a giant anaconda from the Brazilian captain and crewmembers on a bigger boat on my way from Tefé to Manaus. They spoke of the giant anaconda as *Cobra Grande* (Great Snake). As usual, people volunteered to tell me more stories than I expected. Realizing that in the Amazon basin the best repositories of folktales are natives and those who still live in close contact with rivers, trees, and animals, I visited indigenous communities. I also stayed in hotels near ports or marketplaces to be able to inquire about the supernatural from people coming from forests or rivers to sell products, visit relatives, or run errands in town. In those lodges, I would strike up informal conversations with people about the area where they lived. Many times I received invitations to spend a few days in their homes. There, I would partake in their fishing activities, go to their plot gardens and, on a couple of occasions, accompany them on hunting excursions. Whether helping them uproot manioc roots or sitting with them on a tree trunk to take a break, I had the opportunity to listen to tales and see firsthand the way they lived and their aspirations for themselves and their children. I was also able to hear *in situ* their detailed and in depth knowledge of trees, plants, animals, creeks, sounds, and weather. It was an opportunity to learn much more about their land than what is available through television programs, history books, and maps produced by our culture or their governments.

On one of my trips to the city of Iquitos in the Peruvian Amazon, I talked to Doña Corina Rodríguez. She was the owner of a family restaurant, and had spent several years making a living washing clothes for coca leaf gatherers in Tingo María on the Huallaga River. I had trouble sleeping while I was staying in a room at the back of her house, and she explained to me that a *Tunchi*, or spirit of the dead, lived there and didn't like people who stayed in that room. Every night, after I came back from talking to other storytellers in town or in nearby communities, Doña Corina entertained me along with others who came to eat there by telling stories of pink dolphins or *bujeos colorados*. The stories were about female dolphins who would transform into beautiful blonde women and show up at parties in Iquitos on Saturdays. Men would fall madly in love with them. Doña Corina told many other stories as well, including those about the Yanapuma, the Jaguar of the Devil, lupuna trees, and the Chullachaki.

On the outskirts of Iquitos I met Don Manuel Murayari, an urban *vegetalista*, the Spanish name for healers who treat patients with herbs and sacred plants. He was also a shaman and had a clinic where locals with various illnesses came to be treated with medicinal plants and his singing of *icaros* or incantations taught to him by plant spirits and the Chullachaki. The Chullachaki is the spirit of the forest who appeared initially to give him healing powers, "showing up like a little deer with a star on his forehead." Don Manuel Murayari told me about his experience of fasting and obtaining wisdom for healing. He said he was allowed to tell me only superficially how his powers worked.

"There are many things that I can't tell you unless you enter a process of fasting and sexual abstinence," he explained. "No women, no spices, no lard," he advised me. Thanks to him I was able to understand the important role played by hallocinogenic plants like the vine Ayahuasca, *Banisteriopsis caapi*, and other plants used for the same purpose such as Toé, *Brugmansia suaveolens*. I learned through him, and later from other medicine men from the Amazon basin, that by consuming these and other potions from trees and plants and by following special diets, shamans gain access to the worlds where the "mothers" of trees and animals live. There in contact with forest spirits he not only obtained healing powers but also gained knowledge to advise people on their relationships with the natural world. In the Amazon forest where people depend on hunting, fishing, and cutting trees for protein and shelter, and where, according to the myths of indigenous cosmologies, trees and animals are considered people, interactions between human dwellers and "mothers" or "masters" of trees and animals have the potential to become conflictive and when this occurs the mediation of a shaman is needed.

Don Manuel Murayari also told me how he had learned much of his art in Peru and later had continued his studies in São Paulo de Olivença, Brazil, with a great *macumbero*, a practitioner of African religiosity, who was also involved in black arts.

As my interest in listening and gathering folktales grew, I began to take trips to the Amazon each summer and sometimes during winter break. Whether on the Madeira River near Porto Velho, Brazil, Tena, Ecuador, Riberalta, Bolivia, or in San Fernando de Atabapo in Venezuela, the people I met were very much like those I knew from childhood. On the island of Marajo, at the mouth of the Amazon in the Atlantic Ocean, and in Guyana, there lived many descendants of Amazonian-African unions. Through an anthropologist friend who had done extensive fieldwork and lived for a prolonged period in the Ecuadorian Amazon, I met Don Fermín Shiguango and spent time with him and his family at the Cusano River. Walking in the forest, he told me about the medicinal properties of certain plants as he used them in the ritual baths he gave. He told me more about the visionary plant Toé, known among his fellow Ecuadorian shamans as wanduc, *Brugmansia suaveolens*. There it was widely known to have hallucinogenic powers and to be beneficial for treating arthritis, rheumatic pain and cough. Like ayahuasca, wanduc has been used as a visionary plant for thousands of years by indigenous people and is currently used in the Ecuadorian Amazon by shamans for divination and to communicate with forest spirits.

On all my trips, I met native people who had come to live in small settlements and cities as a result of the displacement caused by the presence and pressures of the modern world thirsty for oil, timber, gold, cocaine, and other Amazonian products. I witnessed them roaming the streets of buzzing frontier towns without any sense of belonging in the new places. Their loss of dignity caused by the destruction of the trees and animals considered part of their spiritual world was also evident. Regard for the animals and plants as living feeling beings is a part of their conception of a world as a place where humans are kin to animals and trees. This drastically differs from our Western assumption of humans as masters of the world. Their way of experiencing the world, which results from their religious and ethical attitudes toward the land, entails necessary rules and practices for living intimately with nature while coping with illness, evil human nature and other malaises. If for us in the Western world markers of happiness are the amount of wealth and fame a person is able to amass, for indigenous Amazonians and their descendants it is maintaining healthy social relationships with the natural and spiritual world. Supernatural entities are sources of knowledge that inhabit invisible worlds within the physical realm and share their wisdom with humans. Many natives however, have lost much of their ancestral forests, the necessary and essential dwellings of these spirits who also protect the trees and animals easing the pressure from human activities. A forest dweller in the Brazillian Amazon near Tefé once pointed out to me: "With all the clearing of the land, the Curupira and all the 'mothers' of the trees and animals have gone to live deeper in the forests, but let me tell you, they are still alive, they just have moved away from the noise of chainsaws and people."

In many parts of the basin, the memory of the cruelty brought to Amazonia by the rubber boom is still recounted by elderly storytellers when talking about spirit guardians of the forests. I heard the same tales while growing up in the areas of the Caquetá and Putumayo rivers, where a Peruvian rubber company, known as Casa Arana, had contributed to the enslaving and genocide of thousands of Uitoto indigenous peoples. In my childhood, I heard stories about the rubber boom as told by the elderly father of my friend Alfredo Castro; and in my travels as an adult visiting the abandoned rubber trading post of Cachuela Esperanza, on the Beni River in the Bolivian Amazon, I heard stories about the ruthlessness and wealth of rubber barons.

I was lucky to hear live folktales throughout the region and returned from each trip with notes and recordings of many hours of tales and conversations with Amazonians about their lives. I spent a great deal of time with each of the stories, reconstructing them from multiple fragments, and also pondering how to reconstitute each one as a whole. It is also true that having various fragments and versions of the same story has granted me room for creativity. My written versions are simply one more step in the process through which folktales are born, travel, and change with time. In my attempt to craft individual narratives, instead of presenting the many repetitions found in the raw variants, I have recreated each one as a succinct tale. A poetic approach involving imagery and an avoidance of flowery descriptive prose leaves space for the reader's imagination. To keep the Amazonian flavor and sense of wonder in each story, I have attempted to incorporate and maintain the tone I heard in the original versions. I made an effort to conserve intriguing twists and unexpected endings. It was a privilege for me to witness the moment when the stories were created, as each performance of the same tale morphed into a new story. My objective in each recasting was to trigger in the reader the same awe conveyed by live storytellers

In gathering and recasting these folktales from the living tradition, I attempted to illustrate the unrecorded history of the natural world of Amazonians and the desires and memories of their ancestors, unveiling for us their continuing assumption that trees, animals, and rivers are sentient beings, and that we humans are simply a single part of the world.

The Tales

Forests of giant trees, fabulous animals, and the biodiversity of many species yet to be discovered have not only given rise to the world of extraordinary beings and mysterious plants in indigenous cosmologies, but have also led to interpretation, elaboration, and continuity in the folktales of their descendants and the multiethnic newcomers who came to live in the Amazon basin. These stories, told to children by parents and grandparents, illustrate the importance of reciprocity and regard for nature and reveal codes of good behavior among humans. They combine elements of the ecological practices of native Amazonians, Judeo-Christian conventions for living and other Western themes, and historical transformations enacted by old and new inhabitants coming to the region.

The purpose of this book is to provide the English-speaking audience with a collection of the rich lore of the inhabitants of the Amazon basin. The folktales recast here present the public with a broad spectrum of representative stories from the entire region containing the Amazonian view of their world and themselves. These tales, from a variety of geographical areas of the basin, are constantly adapted with each oral retelling. This collection provides a snapshot of Amazonian folklore in its current variation before new changes are incorporated.

The forty-one stories presented in this book have been thematically grouped into the following categories: tales of origin, tales about anacondas and boas, tales about dolphins and other aquatic seducers, tales of beasts and forest defenders, tales of dark and malevolent shamans, tales of punishment for ill behavior, and tales of special places, plants, and birds.

To facilitate reading, each tale is followed by a paragraph-length note giving additional information on the story or introducing places and peoples of Amazonia where the tale is currently in vogue. The collection contains related illustrations by Jaime Luis Choclote, an artist from the Peruvian Amazon. Photographs, the majority of which were taken by the author over the years of collecting the tales, give a visual representation of people and the places in the Amazon basin where the fieldwork for this collection was done. A map of the basin is included to acquaint readers with the geographical area from which the tales originate. The glossary provides clarification about animals and plants mentioned in the stories.

The tales are woven from the fabric of experiences of fishermen, loggers, rubber tappers, hunters, Amazonian peasants, intruders, and other forest and small settlement dwellers. Supernatural animals and magical entities play important roles in the stories by providing people with gifts, advice, and knowledge of the forest. It is necessary to understand the importance of Amazonian shamans, who appear as characters or are alluded to in many of the tales. As seen in other traditional societies throughout the world, Amazonian shamans are respected in their communities and play a role in the existence of these oral narratives as they interpret events which are subsequently incorporated into the folklore. Many times the shaman is a mestizo who lives in and serves the small settlements. Through their mythical thinking, as they mediate between the human world and the world of the spirits, they give explanations to patients and people about experiences in their daily lives. Thus, plots of Amazonian tales involving questions about encounters with the supernatural, including related disappearances or illnesses, usually convey prescribed consultations with a shaman. It is commonplace to hear scholars and scientists who work in Amazonia say that shamans know so much about medicinal properties of plants that each time a shaman dies, humankind is deprived of a whole library of knowledge.

The book opens with "Tales of Origin," providing the readers with a cosmological sense of the beginning of the Amazon basin. "Moniyamena: The Origin of the Amazon River" renders a mythical explanation for the existence of the Amazon River, the most important topographical feature of the area to Amazonians.

As presented in the second chapter, "Tales about Anacondas and Boas," the anaconda, and the boa constrictor on land—two of the most important mythological figures in all of the regional folk narratives—undergo a variety of transformations in the Amazonian imagination, leading to tales of correspondences and conflict between humans and the natural world as well as playing important roles in the notion of respect for the landscape. In some instances, the anaconda and the boa give advice and have healing powers. However, the anaconda *(Eunectes murinus)* can also become furious and take the form of a Yakumama, a fantastic snake with eyes like the headlights of a truck, and produce an array of atmospheric phenomena. It can tilt the boats of greedy fishermen and people who trespass into her realm, as portrayed in the tale "Yakumama: Mother of All Water Beings." In "Sachamama: Mother of the Forest," the boa constrictor takes the shape of a giant snake on which all forest life grows and turns into a furious earth and sky when intruders encroach.

Stories related to the river and the underwater world involving dolphins, mythical animals, and creatures acting as lovers are grouped in the third chapter, "Tales about Dolphins and Other Aquatic Seducers." Freshwater dolphins are considered supernatural beings that live in modern and fabulous underwater cities. In their recurrent role as seducers, dolphins appear as beautiful blonde men and women who sneak into riverbank settlements and entice humans, as in the tale "María and the Dolphins." Wounding or killing a dolphin and eating its meat are considered taboo by most Amazonians. Characters in the tales who commit such offenses are severely punished, as portrayed in the story "The City of the Dolphins." Scholars, such as Candace Slater (1994, 2002) and Nigel J. H. Smith (1996), believe dolphins' actions, in the Amazonian imagination, are symbolic of relationships between people as well as of sociopolitical tensions and transformations in the region.

Other tales of this lore presented in "Tales of Beasts and Forest Defenders" are about the belief held by Amazonians that plants and animals have guardians or spirit-mothers to defend them. Some of the stories, along with Amazonian native lore, reflect influences of European traditions regarding the observance of certain sacred days. One example is the narrative "Mapinguari: One-Eyed Ogre," about a hideous giant forest monkey and a greedy hunter who disobeys the sacred principle of resting on the Sabbath day to keep it holy. On many occasions, the guardian spirits grant permission for hunting or fishing, but any greed or waste of game can upset them. The most well-known and feared guardian in the forest is a protean figure called *Curupira* in the Brazilian and Colombian Amazon and *Chullachaki* in the Peruvian Amazon. Both act as protectors and are frequently known to trick hunters and cause their victims to become lost in the forest and get ill. Many times, the individual has been punished for his disrespectful behavior or for disobeying the spirit's warning given to hunters or rubber tappers directly or in dreams about killing animals or abusing the rubber trees. Such is the case in the story "Curupira: Guardian Spirit of the Forest" and in "Chullachaki: Owner of Trees and Animals." A tale symbolic of transformations and violence rendered by life in the rain forest and by gender conflict is "Amasanga Warmi: A Ferocious Wife."

While vividly illustrating many aspects of Amazonian life, such as expectations, desires, negotiations with the immediate environment, and relationships among individuals, this collection incorporates stories about human behavior toward others and the vices of individuals. In the fifth chapter, "Tales of Dark and Malevolent Shamans," there are stories about evil shamans committing violent and predatory sorcery as exemplified in "Kanaima: Dark Shamans." There are also tales about those who are able to use magical objects and plants to do harm to people at will. Some stories involve a composite of cultural themes such as Mediterranean patriarchal moral codes imposed on women's behavior as illustrated in "Pusanga: Love Ointment" and "Runamula: Women of Ill Repute Turn into Mules." Tales about good and evil spirits roaming the streets and harming or helping people grouped under "Tales of Punishment for Ill Behavior" are also intended to serve as moral checkpoints to prevent misconduct. Reflecting the influences of European and African traditions in the native lore, punishment for consumption of alcohol, addiction to games, and lasciviousness are presented in stories such as "Lamparilla: Glowing Ghost," "Cowboy Quemdera," and "Caballococha: A Town plagued by Ill Behavior."

The chapter "Tales of Special Places, Plants, and Birds" contains plots constructed from human experiences in extraordinary places or from individual interactions with special, birds, trees, and plants that are inhabited by spirits that give them powers, warn, enlighten, and favor them or at times reprimand them for their faulty actions. Such themes are presented in stories such as "Boa Plants: Plants Turn into Animals," "Chicua: Messenger Bird," and "Pumayuyu: A Plant with Magical Powers."

As in the mythological worlds of most Amazonian indigenous groups, the tales presented in this book include animals, plants, places, and objects that have magical and transformational powers, and changing form can be a central motif. In the folklore of the Amazon, the metamorphosis of a person or plant into an animal, or vice versa, is commonplace. Unlike realist stories of the Western world, the fantastic is rendered as normal in the realm of these tales.

Along with transformation of the landscape, the presence of electric lamps, radios, television, and vehicles in even the most remote areas is causing traditional lore to lose its influence in some regions. However, themes of social relationships between humans and nature persist in the minds of natives, mestizos, loggers, fishermen, and ordinary people. These stories are told and retold while fishing, taking a break in the forest plot gardens, or talking at night by candlelight or oil lamps known as *lamparina*. They persist in small towns and urban areas where they are evident in music, paintings, daily talk, jokes, and other cultural manifestations. This form of entertainment connects the present history and myth of Amazonians, and also carries metaphorical messages exemplary to a new global sense of awareness of environmental preservation that is shared by people from both modern and traditional societies.

Intended Audience and Use for This Book

The folktales in this collection fill the void in libraries for the general audience interested in learning about natural life and culture in the Amazon rain forest. Since the tales reveal lifestyles, traditions, and cultural rules, this collection will be helpful for readers ranging from high school students investigating folklore or cultures, to those conducting research in the humanities and social sciences. College professors and scholars interested in the intersecting fields of Latin American literature and the environment, folk culture, ethnobotany, mythology, religion, and nature, as well as global literatures may also find this collection useful as it is the only existing selection of folktales representative of the entire Amazonian basin. This book is a resource for anyone interested in Amazonian studies.

References

Smith, Nigel J. H. *The Enchanted Amazon Rain Forest: Stories from a Vanishing World.* Gainesville: University of Florida Press, 1996.

Slater, Candace. *Entangled Edens: Visions of the Amazon.* Berkeley: University of California Press, 2002.

———. *The Dance of the Dolphin.* Chicago: University of Chicago Press, 1994.

CHAPTER 1

Tales of Origin

Moniyamena: The Origin of the Amazon River

*O*nce in the forest, food became scarce, and people were hungry. One day, while searching for fruit to take to her family, a girl named Moniyamena ran across a very large earthworm. She was afraid, but when she looked at the earthworm again, he turned into a handsome young man. He said to her, "Moniyamena, I live alone in a place nearby, and if you come to see me every day, I will give you fruits and food for your people."

The girl was very happy with this proposition because she was, in fact, attracted to the boy. From then on, she would come home every day with manioc roots and tasty forest fruit such as pineapples, *copoasú*, *uvillas*, and other delicious foods that he gave her.

One day, the boy and Moniyamena were in a nest of leaves that they had made, when the girl's mother appeared. She said, "Traitor, I have been looking for you everywhere, and I knew I would find you this way." With that, she threw a giant pan of boiling water upon them. The girl covered herself with large leaves from a *platanillo* plant, but the boy could not do so, and he died screaming.

After the death of the boy, food became even more scarce, and everyone in the forest began to suffer from hunger again. Nevertheless, where the boy died, an enormous tree grew, reaching the sky. It produced a great variety of fruits, so the people called it the tree of abundance. Everyone in the forest took food from the tree, and happiness returned to the village.

However, one day, some greedy men came, and they decided to knock down the tree and grab all the fruit for themselves. When they cut down the tree, the entire forest grew dark, and from then on, sadness came to the people. The children of those who cut down the tree walked around desperately and longed for the better days of their parents.

Seeing this, the spirits of the forest said, "These people are suffering. Let's make the tree begin to rot and turn its trunk into the biggest river on earth, with fish and fruit that they can eat." Ever since the spirits did this, nobody has gone hungry again. The river has been in the forest, feeding the animals, the trees, and also the clouds that drink from its waters. The oceans were formed from all the leaves that fell toward the east.

From its branches, the spirit friends formed the Putumayo River, the Caquetá River, the Madeira River, and the other rivers that carry water to the one they call the Amazon.

In the meantime, people say they hope it does not occur to any of those who live in the forest to grab all of the food for themselves.

Tales of an immense tree that reaches the sky and provides an abundance of food are common in the indigenous cosmologies throughout the Amazon region. This version associates the tree with the origin of the river system and reveals the ecological concerns of the area's current inhabitants.

Vitória Régia: Giant Water Lily

$\mathcal{P}$eople tell the story of an indigenous girl who was very beautiful and loved by all. She was quiet and enjoyed taking walks at night, gazing into the sky. One day, she asked her father, who everyone said was as smart as a *pajé* (shaman), if the silvery light of the moon above the giant *samaúma* tree was the reflection of a hearth fire in someone's house.

Her father, who was a very wise chief, told her, "The most courageous warrior lives there. He guards the night, making sure that evil spirits do not steal it."

The girl liked what her father said and fell in love with the warrior. After that, she refused all those who asked for her hand in marriage and searched only for the warrior. She wanted to see him up close and talk to him.

One night, when she saw the moon come out and rise over the big trees, she told her father, "There is the warrior again. Father, I am going to search for him, now that he is close to the earth, before he drifts higher."

She took off running to reach the shining house of the warrior. But the light was far from her and kept rising higher in the sky. The girl ran until she arrived at the shore of a lake at midnight. She was on the verge of fainting, but gathered her strength when she saw the moon in the water. Surely, the warrior would be there.

"Finally, he has heard my cries of love," the girl said, flinging herself toward him to hug him. But the poor girl had bad luck. She fell into the water and drowned.

When her parents and everyone in her village noticed that she was missing, they began searching for the girl. Finally, they discovered her body floating in the lake. She had changed into a beautiful plant whose delicate flower would open its petals at night as if it wanted to see the moon. The tribe cried many tears for the girl. They begged their gods and ancestors that her body would also grow in other parts of the forest, since it had been turned into the beautiful flower now known as Vitória Régia. "May she live in the lakes and waters of the Amazon for a long time, as long as we inhabit the forest."

This giant lily, believed to be capable of sustaining the weight of a person, has a fragrant flower that opens at night. It received its name in tribute to Queen Victoria of England in the nineteenth century. Although some claim that this story comes from the Maués natives who live between the Tapajós and Madeira rivers, multiple variations of this tale exist throughout the Amazon River basin. The present version was gathered in Leticia, Colombia.

CHAPTER 2

Tales about Anacondas and Boas

Huayramama: Snake Mother of the Wind

*E*veryone who knew Don Emilio Shuña agreed that he was a man of great power. His grandparents, who were healers, taught him to use the force of the rivers and the earth by fasting and drinking visionary brews from *yacutoé* and *ayahuasca* plants. But this wasn't enough power for Don Emilio. He also wanted to control the forces of the sky. So he drank tea made from the red *huayracaspi*, the magical tree known to be the mother of the Huayramama. One morning, after nine days of fasting and drinking the magical huayracaspi, Don Emilio saw an enormous boa[1] flying in the wind. She had the face of an old woman with very long hair that tangled in the clouds.

The old woman landed on the roof of his house and said, "OK, man, here I am. What do you want from me?"

Don Emilio said, "I want the power to control the wind and rain and anything else that comes from above."

"I will give you these powers on the condition that you continue fasting for forty-five more days," the Huayramama said. "But watch out for my children; they are evil winds that harm people."

Don Emilio did as she said. After fasting, with the power he received from the Huayramama, Don Emilio could control the wind and rain, serving and curing people who came from far away in the forest—those who were near death because of an evil wind, those who had lost their crops for lack of rain, women tormented by storms, or simply fishermen who could not catch anything because the rivers were too full.

Don Emilio's powers were really tested when evil winds attacked one of the nearby towns. The winds blew so hard that the cows, pigs, and even a few children flew through the air. To help the people, Don Emilio fasted for several days beneath the palm trees while singing the songs that the Huayramama had taught him. Sitting there, drinking his huayracaspi tea and blowing tobacco smoke, he managed to calm the Huayramama's bad children, and sent them to live in the holes under the trees.

In revenge, the evil winds whirled around his house and tried to kill him, but Don Emilio defended himself by driving the winds under the trees. From time to time, the Huayramama would come and put her hand on his head to strengthen his powers. Don Emilio became so strong and so helpful that, during the rainy season, the boys would come to him and say, "Don Emilio, don't let it rain today. We want to play soccer this afternoon."

Then he'd call his wife and ask her to bring him his cigars: "Elena, bring me my *mapachos.*" Cigars in hand, he'd head for his place under the palms to sing the Huayramama's songs, and everything would be fine.

But, as good things never last, one day, Don Emilio didn't wake up. Some people blamed jealous sorcerers, enemies of his who lived on the other side of the river; others said it had been the evil winds. No one knows for sure, but what is certain is that the townspeople and those in the forest cried for him. They had to wait a few days to bury him because Don Emilio had asked to be buried under the roots of the red huayracaspi in the middle of the forest.

"I want to be buried there because that tree is my mother," he had said.

Amazonians tell stories about supernatural snakes that teach and give power to humans. Other snakes who give power include the Sachamama (Boa constrictor) and the Yakumama (Eunectes murinus), snake mothers and guardians of the earth and water. Oral narratives such as this about the Huayramama's powers are common in the Peruvian Amazon, especially among the inhabitants surrounding the Ucayali River.

---

[1] **Boa:** The terms "boa" and "anaconda" are used interchangeably in Spanish-speaking Amazonia, although technically, an anaconda (*Eunectus murinus*) is a water reptile, while the boa (*Boa constrictor*) lives on land.

Sachamama: Mother of the Forest

Years ago, during the rubber boom, a man and his wife collected the latex of the rubber trees to bring to the depot by the river. One day, when they were carrying balls of *shiringa*, an Amazonian term for rubber, they decided to camp beside the trunk of an enormous fallen tree. The woman cut a few shrubs whose roots were covering the trunk. When she cut them, she saw the trunk bleeding, and told her husband, "Look, this trunk bleeds like an animal."

The man answered, "Don't worry, woman. This tree must have red sap."

The couple went to the river, delivered the rubber balls, and returned. On the way back, they decided to camp in the same place, and built a fire. As they did, they saw the shrubs and trees shaking. It was as if an earthquake were coming out of the fallen tree and the shrubs.

Then it began to rain very hard. The rain put out the fire, and the trees calmed down.

The next day, the man and woman noticed that the trunk and shrubs had vanished. In their place was a wide road. When they saw this, the man asked his wife, "How is it possible that, year after year, we have walked this path, and now all the trees have disappeared?"

The woman replied, "This is a bad sign. We had better get out of here."

They returned home and tried to forget what they had seen. Nevertheless, the man could not stop thinking about the trees that had disappeared. He was so overcome with curiosity that he told his wife he was going to try to find out what had happened to the giant trunk that had vanished along with all the other trees. His wife begged him not to do it because that tree surely concealed a mystery.

"Just thank God that nothing happened," she said.

The man then consulted a shaman, who explained that that trunk must have been the Sachamama, the mother of the forest. "The Sachamama doesn't like intruders. She likes to live in one place but sometimes moves; she probably isn't there anymore." Stubbornly, the man went looking to see where the fallen tree and the Sachamama might

---

have gone. He walked along the wide road that he and his wife had seen. When he got to its end, he found himself in a dark place. He felt lost, so he lit the place with his flashlight. It was then he saw a big pile of animal and human bones. "Impossible!" The man thought, "There's no place where all the animals go to die." He considered returning home, but again his curiosity got the better of him, and he went looking farther away from the pile of bones.

Eventually, he saw the trunk, which grew larger as he got nearer, and then he found a meadow with a brook illuminated by the sun. He heard the singing of a *chicua*, a bird whose presence was considered an omen. He saw some ducks; and then a deer came and stood motionless as if it were stuck to the ground. Then a tapir appeared and the same thing happened. He noticed how both animals, as if hypnotized, were headed toward the opening of a cave at the end of the meadow. At that moment, the man realized that the first thing he had seen was the rear end of a monster, and in front was a mouth it used to eat animals and people. The monster must have been an immense boa that attracted the animals with its hypnotic powers.

The man started to feel dizzy. To avoid falling into a trance, he cut through the beast's spell with his machete. Since the beast realized it couldn't get him with its magnetism, it came closer to him. It raised its gigantic head, and under its neck the man saw a big blade like a bulldozer. At that moment, the shrubs and trees around him started to shake. Now the man wanted only to escape. He ran behind the monster, looking for the wide road on which he had arrived. While he was running, he saw what had seemed to be a fallen tree covered with fungi that had big scales like stone plates. It was the Sachamama, just as the shaman had told him and as the natives described her. The man returned home and told the story to his wife.

In her wisdom, she responded, "Don't doubt that you saw the Sachamama, the mother of the forest, and all her trees and animals. The best thing you can do is never go to such places, looking for what you haven't lost."

Many stories from woodcutters and hunters in the Peruvian Amazon relate the Sachamama's actions with people traveling through the forest during the rubber boom. They also say that the Sachamama's rain and lightning often causes fevers and strong headaches to hunters and other intruders. Such illnesses can be cured only by treatment from a shaman using chants and tobacco smoke.

Yakumama: Mother of All Water Beings

*A*man who had worked for many years in the forest decided to return to the city of Iquitos. He was going down the Napo River with his family, servants, fine wood, and animals, when a storm broke. Native fishermen fleeing to the shore made signals that he should come to their village to wait out the storm because the Yakumama, the mother of the river and all living things in it, must be around.

The man didn't want to wait; he told his wife to get her rosary and pray to God to placate the storm. The woman prayed and prayed, but this accomplished nothing. The couple soon found themselves spinning in a whirlpool that threatened to destroy their boat and the cargo raft. Then the man's indigenous servants began saying the place was haunted. They threw food and *aguardiente* (sugarcane liquor) into the river, and the whirlpool let them go.

However, instead of seeking refuge, the man commanded that the group continue their trip. Once they were back in the main channel of the river, the bad weather returned. Native people appeared and advised them not to go on. Suddenly, a squall bigger than all the others came, and the river started to fill with a bluish fog. The group saw some trees filled with monkeys, sloths, and other animals that moved as if they were navigating, trying to get to a safer place. Eventually, the blue fog became so sticky and dark that the travelers couldn't continue. There they were, in the middle of the river, with a terrible storm raging around them.

Fearful of the river, the man allowed his servant to sing and puff tobacco smoke to calm the elements. But nothing calmed down. There was lots of lightning, and some waves lifted the boat and stuck it in the branches of a big *capirona* tree on the river-bank. The cargo raft was at the mercy of the waters. From the tree, they saw an immense anaconda snake with blue scales on her body; her eyes looked like the lights of a boat. She was moving up and down in the water carrying the *Yaras*, the fish women from the underwater world. The people in the tree branches could hear their laughter.

After gobbling up some trees, the anaconda, her mouth like a magnet, attacked the cargo raft with its fine woods, cows, and pigs. The servants and even the dogs wept to see all the cargo disappear down the anaconda's mouth. The giant snake ate more trees and a small island before she disappeared. Early in the morning, the moon and some stars returned to their places in the sky. The people saw the trees going back to their places like islands. Their eyes hurt from the sticky blue fog, and their bodies itched.

They pulled their boat down from the capirona tree and looked for the village of the natives they had seen the day before. The natives gave them food and invited them to sit by the fire. The man regretted that he had traveled under such conditions and told the villagers about his misfortune, describing the immense anaconda that had gulped down the work of several years. He told them about the Yaras and the trees like islands full of animals.

The villagers told him that the Yakumama lived around that place and that the same had happened to other travelers.

"She gets angry with us, too," they said. "Sometimes, she gets all the fish in her belly and goes to the bottom where she buries herself, and then we can't catch anything. At other times, she goes up into the sky and swirls around and causes so much rain that all the *yuca* (manioc root) and fruits are damaged, and even our canoes sink. But when she is in a good mood, she allows us to fish all we want, and our children, pigs, and chickens grow fat with the corn, plantains, and yuca. She changes all the time," they told him. "Usually, we don't know what we have done to make her so angry."

Stories about an angered Yakumama, told mostly by fishermen and riverine dwellers in the Peruvian Amazon, belong to a body of narratives about the anaconda present in indigenous cosmologies. The anaconda is seen as the mother of water in Amazonia. (In the great variety of anaconda tales throughout the region, the anaconda is also called Puragua in Peru and Cobra Grande in Brazil). According to river dwellers, the Yakumama has almost dissapeared from rivers and lakes due to the excessive presence of ships and outboard motors.

Chapter 2: Tales about Anacondas and Boas

Juan Boa: The Man Who Turned into a River Serpent

*O*ne day, a man named Juan and his sister were traveling in a canoe, when suddenly the river swallowed them up. Their family and friends searched for them in vain. A few days later, the man appeared to his mother in a dream and said, "Mother, don't search for me anymore; I have turned into a water boa and live in the Amazon. I spend my time traveling from the upper Ucayali River to Santarem, back and forth."

His family and friends got used to his absence.

One day, when Juan was traveling near Manaus, he entered a very dark place he took to be the Negro River. In reality, he was entering the mouth of an enormous *pirarucú*, the biggest fish in the Amazon. Further upstream, he met up with a giant leech; each time he tried to pass, the leech stuck to his body. He tried to kill the leech but couldn't; it was very big.

Once again, the man returned to speak with his mother in her dreams and said, "Although I'm happy to be alive, I'm beginning to tire of this way of life. Please help me get out of the river." So the mother and her other children tried to retrieve him with the help of a shaman who was an expert in rescuing those that the dolphins and the Yakurunas, spirits from the underwater world, took to live with them beneath the water. The shaman used charms called *icaros*, but nothing worked. Juan continued to live in the river.

One day, he was attacked by another boa, which happened to be his very own sister. She had become a giant boa and was traveling with a strong male boa who had convinced her to kill her brother so that they could be the rulers of the Amazon.

Juan defended himself successfully, and ended up killing them both.

He continued traveling from one place to another without knowing what to do or where to go. He wanted to stop for a while and rest in a place that seemed to be a big beach. But the beach began to move, and Juan realized that it was a giant stingray that had stopped to take a nap on the shore. So he continued on his way. When he saw an island full of trees laden with fruit and birds, he stopped again. The island was really a big turtle that had decided to leave the very same day of his arrival. Once again, poor Juan had to leave suddenly.

He continued upstream, but he became so tired and hungry that he decided to stop where a garrison of soldiers guarded the river. He thought to himself, "I am going to see if I can find someone to help me." However, a soldier took aim at him with a loaded machine gun.

Juan cried out, "Please don't shoot me. I'm a man. I was turned into a boa when I fell into the river. I worked as a logger in Atacuari where I lived with my mother and brothers and sisters." Then he told the soldier that he would become a man again if someone shot him directly in the star on the middle of his forehead, and he begged the soldier to shoot straight. "Aim carefully. Shoot right in the middle of the star. Don't miss or you might kill me."

The soldier told him not to worry.

They waited until night, and Juan got back into the river to gain speed, then reemerged and headed toward the soldier. He moved so fast that he looked like the river itself. The soldier wasn't afraid; he didn't move from his post because he knew that it was Juan. Nevertheless, when he fired, he missed, and the bullet hit Juan in an eye. He writhed in the water, and his skin began to peel off his body and floated down the river. He was freed from being a boa and emerged from the water. He only had one eye left, but he was still very grateful to the soldier.

After returning to his family, Juan sadly told them what had happened to his sister.

Afterward, remembering his time as a snake, he would say to his friends: "I tell you, I would never have imagined personally running into giant leeches, stingrays, enormous turtles, or any such strange animals in this river. In fact, I was very lucky."

This is one of the numerous versions of stories about anacondas and other aquatic creatures capable of transforming into humans, or humans who turn into aquatic creatures. Told by fishermen in the area of Puerto Nariño in the Colombian Amazon, this version appears to be a variation of the Cobra Norato story well-known among people in small towns in the Brazilian Amazon. In such tales, Norato, the son of a human mother and a serpent father, is wounded by a soldier to be returned to his human state.

CHAPTER 3

Tales about Dolphins and Other Aquatic Seducers

María and the Dolphins

*O*n the banks of the Amazon near the town of Leticia lived a girl named María who washed clothes every morning. While working, she liked to watch the pink dolphins jump and play in the water. They were the same color as the face of the handsome young man who had been appearing lately in her dreams. He sang words of love accompanied by beautiful guitar music: "María, if you love me, I will take you to live in a marvelous city where you will always be happy. At our wedding, you will have beautiful jewelry and a dress that will outshine the scales of the *tucunaré* fish."

One morning, a dolphin that had been playing with the others began to swim back and forth, moving very close to her. She decided to play with the dolphin, so she asked him to bring her a fish. "Why don't you bring me a *gamitana* fish?" she asked.

The dolphin swam off and came back with the fish she had requested. Then he brought her another, and another. Meanwhile, she heard the same music that was in her dreams coming from the water. Finally, there were so many gamitanas that they filled her laundry basket, so she told the dolphin to stop.

From then on, every time María went to wash clothes, she found the playful dolphin waiting for her close to the shore. Also, the man from her dreams started to pass by her house at night. He was a handsome young man with gleaming white teeth; he dressed well and wore gold chains around his neck. Sometimes at night she would see him from her house standing by a *yarumo* tree holding a bouquet of reeds.

María's father didn't approve of this young man standing around and looking for his daughter without first coming to the house to ask permission. But each time María's father tried to confront the boy, he would vanish. The father noticed, however, that the boy's tracks always disappeared near the water. He also noticed that when María rode in the canoe during the day, many dolphins would jump and play around her as if they wanted to greet her.

María's life went on. She continued to hear the same music coming from somewhere in the river, and at night she dreamed of the young man with the brilliant smile and skin the color of the pink dolphins. She lost interest in taking canteens full of manioc brew to the young men who worked in the garden patches and admired her. Because her young lover continued to come by the house, especially when her father was away,

María's mother told her to stop going to the river. A shaman had warned her about the many young girls who were stolen by dolphins. "They come disguised as handsome men and take the girls to live with them in the palaces they have at the bottom of the river," her mother repeated.

To prevent this from happening, María's parents took her to live in a settlement far away from the river. "Thank God," said her parents, "No dolphin comes around the house to bother her anymore." They were pleased that in their new town, any boy who wanted to meet her asked permission from her father first. But María didn't want to marry any young man from that town, and one day she vanished without a trace. Thinking that she had gotten lost in the forest, her parents hired hunters to search, but none of them found her.

The people all talked about her, and one of her young suitors said, "I bet María married that pink dolphin who used to smile at her; now she must be living at the bottom of the Amazon near Leticia."

In many parts of the Amazon, pink dolphins (Inia geoffrensis) *are associated with white people or with foreigners—to the point that in some places, they are referred to as "gringos." In the different versions of stories from women in a charitable nursing home and fishermen in Leticia, Colombia, dolphins transform themselves into rich men. It is common that the narrators in almost all areas of the Amazon embellish their tales with descriptions of the luxuries and lifestyles of the Western world that the dolphins enjoy at the bottom of the rivers.*

The Girl and the Anaconda

*O*nce upon a time, there was a girl who lived with her family near a pond that was full of fish and *aguaje* palm trees. Every day, she went to the pond and walked in waist-deep water collecting fruit from the palms. Some afternoons, she would sit sadly on a tree trunk on the banks of the pond, feeling lonely. She didn't know that in that very place, there lived an anaconda that had fallen in love with her.

One day, the snake appeared in the form of a handsome young man. He began courting the girl, and she fell so in love with him that each day, she spent more and more time with him. Every day at noon, she would go to the pond and knock three times on a gourd to call him—toc-toc-toc. Then she waded into the pond, and the young man wrapped himself around her waist. The two would lie embracing each other until dusk. Every day, the girl returned home with aguaje fruit that she had collected and with many fish that the anaconda had given her.

Her parents and little brothers and sisters were very pleased, and they asked how she always managed to get such delicious fish. The girl replied that she caught them with hooks and nets forgotten by a fisherman that she found on her way to the pond.

But her older brother didn't believe her.

He followed her and secretly watched her call the anaconda with the gourd. After a few days, her brother took the gourd and went to the pond with some neighbors. He called the anaconda himself—toc-toc-toc. When the anaconda heard the three knocks of the gourd, he thought it was the girl, and stuck his head above the water.

The brother and his friends shot at him with spears and guns.

The next morning, when the girl called her lover, the anaconda did not appear. She looked and looked, until finally she found his dead body floating in the pond. The girl was heartbroken. She went back to her mother, crying and confessing everything about her anaconda lover, and the fish she had been bringing home. She also confessed to her mother that she was pregnant.

The people of the settlement wanted to condemn her to live alone in the deep forest, but the girl's parents took pity on her and allowed her to live with them. Nine

---

months later, she gave birth to several very pretty little anacondas. Hearing the little anacondas crying like humans, her parents were glad they hadn't kicked her out of the house. They built little wooden boxes for cradles and helped their daughter raise them until they were old enough to live in the pond. If at any time the little anacondas got hungry and cried, the young woman would go to the banks of the pond to feed them.

Some time passed, and the anacondas were eventually able to survive on their own, but they never forgot their mother. Every morning, she and her family would find fresh fish piled in the family's dugout near the shore. The family was delighted with these gifts from the grown-up anacondas.

This all happened long ago. Nowadays, people don't allow their daughters to go alone to the nearby rivers and ponds, for they say they don't want to take care of children who don't look like humans.

Variations of this story were obtained from people on the banks of the Amazon River in Colombia, fishermen near the mouth of the Napo River, and from storytellers in the zone of the Ucayali River in Peru. The premise for this tale is the belief that anacondas, dolphins, and frogs can impregnate women who have contact with the water these animals pass through.

A Gift from Yara, an Underwater Seducer

A young man from Lima, Peru, wanted to make his fortune in the Amazon and came to the Manú River to harvest timber. He started a camp and hired workers from the region. One afternoon, when the workers were either gone for supplies or in the forest marking out the best mahogany trees, the young man found himself alone at the camp. A beautiful girl with green eyes and a face whiter than cotton walked in front of his hut and smiled at him.

He tried to talk to her, but she disappeared.

That night, music from the river woke him. He got up to find out what was going on, but when he went to the river, he heard only the sound of the water washing against its banks. He went home and fell back to sleep, but the music woke him again. Once more, he went to the river, but there was no one there. The third time he was disturbed by music, he thought, "I won't get up; there's nothing there." He stayed in bed, unable to fall asleep.

After awhile, the sound of the music changed into the sound of someone coming out of the water, and he heard footsteps approaching his hut. Thinking it might be the girl, he wanted to go outside to meet her; but all the stories told by his workers about the people of the water who would come to steal men and women ran through his mind, and he decided not to move. Instead, he grew very frightened (something he regretted for the rest of his life) and he stayed glued to his bed, grasping the cross he wore on a chain around his neck. He heard the footsteps going around the house, and he grabbed a dolphin-tooth charm that a friend had given him. Only then he was able to go to sleep.

Toward dawn, the man woke again. He heard something like an animal flopping on the ground and soft guitar and violin music coming from the river. He looked through the crack of the door and saw a lovely fish writhing on the dry dirt of the yard. The fish was a *dorado*, and he wanted to catch it, but he grew fearful, and again stayed put.

The fish's death agonies continued; then the sounds stopped and the music faded.

When his workers returned, the man told them what had happened. They explained that surely it was the Yara, the beautiful seducer from the underwater world who had

---

come to charm him. "What stopped her was the dolphin tooth you wear on your neck," one of the natives who worked for him said. "But, sir, now that you have seen the Yara, it will be very hard for you to fall in love with another woman, no matter to what city or country you go."

"What was that fish jumping out there in front of the house?" asked the young man.

"Well, that was the Yara's gift for your breakfast. You should have grabbed it. It would have brought you good luck, sir."

Stories about blonde-, green-, or blue-eyed women who live at the bottoms of rivers and come out to charm men with their beauty and songs are common throughout Amazonia. In many tales, they are believed to inhabit fantastic underwater cities. Their features, typical of Caucasian females, reflect the influence of European culture on Amazonian indigenous lore already populated with female aquatic seducers. A version of this story was documented and published by Arturo Burga Freitas in 1939.

Yakuruna: Male Lover from the Underwater World

A family that lived on the Napo River had three beautiful daughters. One day, the mother sent the oldest one to fetch water from the river, and she disappeared. When the family asked a shaman for help, he said she had been taken by the people of the water. With the help of a potion of *ayahuasca* and *toé*, two magical plants, the shaman transformed himself into a dolphin and went looking for the girl at the bottom of the river. He returned with the news that the girl was going to marry a Yakuruna[1] down there, one of those handsome men with his face turned backward who share underwater cities with pink dolphins, yaras, and others.

1

"But I will try to bring her back," the shaman promised.

The mother said, "It's not fair. I took good care of her, hoping that one of the merchants or wood buyers from Iquitos would marry her, not so that she would be stolen by the people from the water."

Worried that other Yakurunas would fall in love with her other daughters, the mother told them, "Stay away from the river. You saw what happened to your sister."

The shaman, who was famous among shamans, spent several days by the river smoking tobacco and singing incantations in order to retrieve the stolen girl. Finally, the girl emerged from the river and went to her house. The plastic barrettes that she had been wearing when she vanished were missing. Instead, she had her hair arranged with colorful little fish. When her parents saw her, they were delighted. "Ah, for God's sake, little daughter, where have you been?" cried the mother, and the dogs whined.

The girl told them she was happy; she had missed them, but the world down there was better. "They have cows, chickens, and pigs. There, people don't pay electric or water bills. They also grow manioc, corn, rice and coca, and the plants grow so big that people hardly have to work at all."

Her father marveled at all this, and her mother and sisters listened with awe and admired her fine clothes made of lovely fabric. While they felt her dress, she told them:

"I'm going to marry a Yakuruna and he'll take me to live in a bigger city far away in Brazil." She told her mother that she couldn't stay out of the water long because the air they were breathing was bad, and she ran to the river. Her father chased her, but when he had almost caught her near the shore, the river, which always obeyed the Yakurunas, sent up a great wave and took her away.

The parents became even more vigilant with their remaining daughters, but they still yearned for their oldest girl. Again they went to the shaman, and begged him to go to the underwater city to get her. He fasted and went again to visit the people of the water, but soon returned to tell her parents that she was already the wife of a Yakuruna. Hearing this, they became very sad.

The shaman reassured them, telling them not to worry because she was living very well. He told them stories about life in the underwater world and started to describe the house made of shells and coral. He mentioned the women, half-fish, who were her servants. "There's a whole life down there," said the shaman, "beautiful anacondas serve as hammocks, little turtles are their shoes, and tiny crabs are used as watches. There are curtains made of blue butterflies and fireflies and so many more things that I can't remember."

This made the girl's parents feel better, but the sisters, who were also listening spellbound, secretly wished that some day the same thing could happen to them.

The Yakuruna is a creature thought to take care of fish and animals at the bottoms of rivers. Since the Yakuruna is believed to fall in love with humans, disappearances of people who live along the riverbanks are blamed on the Yakuruna, as evidenced in this story. It is believed that people kidnapped by Yakurunas are gradually converted into Yakuruna spirits. Those who are kidnapped and return require treatment by a shaman.

[1]**Yakuruna:** Yakuruna means "water-person" in the Kichwa language spoken in some parts of Amazonia.

The City of the Dolphins

Once in the area of Santo Antônio do Içá, Brazil, there was a fisherman who had been on the Amazon River since before dawn without catching even a sardine. He was so frustrated that when he saw a pink dolphin playing by his dugout, he relieved his anger by spearing it. The dolphin screamed in pain but was able to escape by breaking the spear.

The fisherman went back to his village and decided to spend the afternoon and the next day repairing one of his nets. As he was doing this, a speedboat came to his house with two policemen from Santo Antônio do Içá on board. They told the man they had come with a summons to take him to the judge.

"Why?" the poor man asked. "I haven't done anything wrong."

His wife and his children begged the policemen, "Please don't take him away from us," for they would have a hard time without him.

The policemen said they were just following orders. The man gave in and asked his wife to put some dried fish and tobacco in his bag.

In the boat with the policemen, the fisherman noticed that they weren't going toward areas that he was familiar with; the boat wasn't headed to Santo Antônio do Içá as they had told him. He started to worry and noticed that the policemen, instead of having clubs hanging from their belts, wore some long shiny fish he didn't recognize. At this point, the man was about to jump overboard, when suddenly the boat began to sink to the bottom of the river. The man was astonished—they had passed through a mosquito net-like fence without breaking it, and he was completely dry!

They came upon a city like one in the movies.

At the bottom of the river, the lights of cars and stores illuminated the darkness. The man saw dolphin couples in parks, playing with their children in glowing fountains. Then, the dolphin policemen told him that they were hungry, and they went to a restaurant. The policemen ordered raw fish and told the fisherman that if he wanted, he could order something, too. The policemen took off their hats to eat, and the fisherman noticed that they were looking more and more like the dolphins from the river—they were breathing through holes on the top of their heads.

When they left the restaurant, the man looked up and saw the stars and lights of a passenger boat going upstream toward Benjamin Constant, a town on the Amazon River. Later, the policeman took him to a hospital, where many doctors looked at him as if they already knew who he was. There lay the dolphin he had speared, moaning and cursing.

The policemen told the fisherman that he must cure the dolphin, or at least tell the doctors what kind of metal had been used to make the spear. "If he dies," the dolphins told him, "you will have to stay here in jail and then in our city. We dolphins are also people, even though all of you who live up there don't believe it."

The poor fisherman became very frightened. He didn't know what to do and began to suffer, thinking about his family. He knew they would be looking for him at this moment on the banks of the Amazon, fearing he had drowned. The man became sad thinking about this. Suddenly, he remembered that dolphins hate tobacco smoke. As soon as the policemen left him alone, the fisherman lit his tobacco. When the dolphins smelled the smoke, everyone in the hospital began to panic.

Doctors ran out shouting for the policemen to take the man away. "Please," they begged, "take that monkey out of here and far from the city, for he is going to kill us all with his smoke."

So, the policemen put the fisherman in a boat and quickly left the city. Once they came to the surface of the river, the dolphin police left the fisherman on an island. There, the man was picked up by some people on a boat coming up from Tefé. He was returned home.

When they saw he was alive, his wife and relatives were happy. Everyone celebrated.

After that, whenever the fisherman went to Santo Antônio do Içá, he would get drunk and shout, "*Os botos são como a gente!* Dolphins are like people! Dolphins are like people!" But the townsfolk didn't believe such stories and made fun of him.

This story, told by fishermen from Benjamin Constant to Tefé on the Amazon River, is one of many varied tales of human aggression toward pink dolphins and dolphins' revenge. Even though dolphins are respected within indigenous cosmologies, the

fisherman's anger toward them in this tale could be attributed to their tendency to destroy fishing nets to steal the catch. This story shows the humanity of dolphins who feel and complain as if they were people that is present in many indigenous oral narratives. It also reveals the ritual use of tobacco to ward off harm, a common practice in the Amazon.

Mawaris: Aquatic Abductors

*C*lose to San Carlos on the Negro River in the Venezuelan Amazon there lived a young man who saved the money he earned collecting oil from *copaíba* trees and gum from *balatá* trees in order to have enough money to get married. One Sunday, the young man was returning from a visit to his girlfriend; he was paddling his canoe around the next-to-last bend in the river before his house. He saw on the banks many pink dolphins, which the people from San Carlos called *toninas*. He drew close, but they disappeared. As he started to paddle on, he heard someone calling him from behind—"Psst, psst, psst."

On the bank, he saw his girlfriend, and she said, "Don't be afraid, it's me. Get the canoe over here and take me with you. I want to go with you right now."

So the young man went over to the riverbank, the girl got in, and they started paddling to where he lived. But before they arrived, the girl threw herself into the river. The young man had to jump in after her. When he finally regained his senses, he found himself in the city of the Mawaris, where there are enchanted people who as adults are able to live in or out of the water and change into an animal, a person, or anything else. The one who had said she was his girlfriend was really a tonina who, because she had fallen in love with him, had tricked him into staying with her. The man had become a dolphin, and now they were going to have Mawari children. Together they ate fish that the Mawaris liked and had a good life under the water.

But the young man still remembered his old life on land, and when there weren't any Mawaris around, he missed it. He could hear from far away the roosters crowing and the dogs barking at his house. He even heard the voices of his parents, who were looking for him in the deepest part of the river because they feared he had drowned. He also heard the chants of the *sacacas*, or healers, trying to find him. One day, he made out the voice of his girlfriend, who was still waiting for him.

The man became so sad that he begged the Mawaris to let him return to his home on land. At first they denied his request, saying that he was already a Mawari, and was therefore unable to go back. But the man begged them repeatedly, and finally they gave in. They let him go on the condition that any children that he fathered would be like them.

So the man returned to land where he rejoined his girlfriend and they got married. Time passed, and as the people of the water had told him, the children that he and his wife had looked like the Mawaris he had lived with at the bottom of the river. They were blond with fair skin, they had no belly buttons, and their bones wouldn't harden. They didn't understand anything in the world, and passed their time silently in the corners. They were, in fact, Mawaris; and when they were at the riverbanks, they talked to the water, as if the water and whatever was beneath it were human, or as if they could see what others could not see—or so said whoever noticed.

The man loved his children, but his wife didn't feel the same. She didn't know about her husband's promise to the Mawaris; and she was sad that her children weren't normal. Finally, the man could not keep his secret any longer and confessed to his wife. Afterward, she became even sadder, and she actually began to dislike her Mawari children.

In the end, to be fair, her husband accepted her leaving him and having normal children with a neighbor.

As for the Mawari children, since they were still young, the man took care of them and later went with them to live under the river. They moved to Temendawí, a city in Brazil, which was the capital of the Mawaris.

Many variations of this story told by market vendors, elderly peasants, and high school teachers from San Fernando de Atabapo in the Venezuelan Amazon, are comparable to tales about the kidnappings by Yakurunas in Peru. In the present story as well as in those told in the Brazilian Amazon, the sacacas are the ones who communicate with the spirits. It is said that, if necessary, they can travel, body and soul, along the bottoms of rivers to find their victims.

Yara: Fish-Woman from the Underwater World

*O*ne day, a woman who lived with her husband's family told her mother-in-law, "Watch my children while I go to the *chacra,* or small plot garden, to find something for lunch." Her mother-in-law agreed and stayed home, telling stories to entertain the children.

The woman was gone for some time. When she returned, in addition to the fruits and *palmitos,* or hearts of palm she had gone for, she also had some delicious fish such as *pintadillos* and *pacus.* When her mother-in-law asked her where such good-looking fish came from, she told her, "I ran into some fishermen who gave them to me."

Later, the woman went to where the children were playing and asked, "Are these my children?"

To which her mother-in-law answered, "Woman, I have taken very good care of your children. I haven't traded them away."

The woman laughed and went into the kitchen to make lunch before her husband got home from work.

While they were eating, her husband asked, "Woman, where did you get this delicious fish? We've never had it before."

"Well," she answered, "It's my special present for you." She added that some neighbors who were fishermen had given the fish to her. The man felt very fortunate to have such a good woman in the kitchen and such generous neighbors.

Later that afternoon, the mother-in-law proposed that they take the children to play in the river while they washed clothes. But the woman replied that she didn't want to go—she had already spent a lot of time in the water. The mother-in-law thought to herself, "I too spend a great deal of time at the river washing clothes and fishing, and I don't complain. This woman isn't acting like herself today." Nevertheless, preferring to avoid problems, she didn't say anything. She spent the whole day by the river washing clothes and making sure that her little grandchildren didn't stray too far from the shore. Still, she worried about her daughter-in-law's behavior, and the old lady told her son that he should watch the woman closely during the night.

Eventually, they all went to sleep. After midnight, the husband, who had been awake all night long, saw his wife get out of bed very quietly and sneak out of the house. The man was enraged because he was sure that she was betraying him with another man, so he followed her as she walked toward the river. But instead of seeing her with another man, he saw her sliding slowly into the calm waters by the shore. As she began to swim, her legs turned into a fish tail. This was not his wife, but a Yara: a creature half woman and half snake that lives in the water and sometimes falls in love with the men along the river.

Now the man was very afraid, and he ran to wake up his friends and neighbors. Since they knew that this creature was not his wife but a Yara, they all agreed to go with their machetes, spears, and guns to find it. By the light of the moon, they found the animal, still wearing a woman's clothes, and killed it.

Later, the unfortunate man's mother explained, "Now you know that your wife is dead and that this animal that wanted to live with you surely killed her yesterday in the chacra."

The man loved his wife very much. He didn't want to believe his mother, so he went running to the chacra where she had last been. When he and his neighbors got there, they found the naked lifeless body of his wife, whose clothes the Yara had stolen.

Loggers who come to buy supplies for their long periods of work in the deep forest and fishermen in the area of the Amazon and Yavari rivers near the border of Brazil and Colombia tell stories about beautiful women who live underwater and come ashore looking for human companionship. These women are very similar to the mermaids from the classical world that tempted Odysseus. In most stories, the Yara is depicted as having a woman's shape; however, in this one, she is presented as having the shape of a mermaid, or Mãe d' água, similar to women fish present in many indigenous oral traditions.

The Dolphin's Children

Once there was a couple that lived on the banks of the Amazon and owned a little store where they sold hooks and salt to fishermen. Whenever the husband went to Leticia or Iquitos to buy more supplies, the woman went to the river to fetch water or catch fish. Sometimes while she was fishing, one of the pink dolphins playing close to the bank jumped near her and called to her with cries that sounded almost human. Later, more dolphins appeared in her dreams, and she could see herself walking in a beautiful underwater city where handsome men and women lived, some of them with dolphin faces.

One day, the husband had to go to Atacuari for some time; while he was gone, a friendly dolphin became even more playful with the woman. In fact, one afternoon he stayed so close to her that she could not fish in peace, and had to chase him away with a stick.

After she went to bed that night, she thought she heard footsteps. It was as if someone were walking around the house wearing rubber boots and wet clothes. This happened for several nights in a row. Once, she thought she even sensed someone in her room. Whenever she managed to fall asleep, she dreamed of living in the city of the dolphins.

A short time later, the woman began to feel sick to her stomach and had very strange pains in her body that would not stop, even with the herb tea that the Cocama healer, or *sabedor*, advised her to take. "I have always been a very healthy person," she thought, "What could be happening to me?"

She asked her sister-in-law about the aches and told her about the dreams and everything else. Her sister-in-law thought the best thing to do was to ask an old Cocama healer. He said that a dolphin had impregnated her, and that there was nothing she could do. The poor woman was distraught, for she loved her husband and she knew he would not believe what had happened.

When her husband returned, he flew into such a rage that if his own mother hadn't been present, he might have killed his wife. He left her and went to live in Leticia, where he took to drinking. His wife cried over losing her husband, but her sister-in-law came to visit whenever she could. When the woman gave birth, instead of having a baby, she had two beautiful dolphins.

"They were dolphins and humans at the same time," her sister- and mother-in-law told everyone.

The Cocama healer advised the woman to return the dolphins to the water. Otherwise, the air would give them a rash and they would die before they were three months old. The Cocama also told her that she must leave them at the banks where she had seen the dolphins jumping. The woman's sister- and mother-in-law wrapped the little dolphins in towels and took them to the river.

That night, the woman dreamed again of the men and women in the city of dolphins. In the dream, one of them thanked her for the return of his children.

This story, heard in Leticia, Colombia, is a good example of dolphin tales in relation to unexplained human pregnancies. According to some indigenous mythologies from the Ucayali region, dolphins are believed to visit women while they are asleep. Referring to the capacity of dolphins to deceive people and to their seductive powers, this story also reveals the Mediterranean masculine honor code that has a notorious influence on the relationships between men and women in the Amazonian world.

CHAPTER 4

Tales of Beasts and Forest Defenders

Mapinguari: One-Eyed Ogre

*N*ear Tefé, on the banks of the Amazon River in Brazil, there was a man who loved hunting so much that he went almost every day of the year. One Sunday, he told his wife, "I'm going to a place where the hunting is good."

"It would be better to wait until tomorrow," his wife said. "It's not good to hunt on Sunday."

"*No domingo também se come.* One must also eat on Sundays," the man said as he grabbed his rifle and left.

On his way to the forest, the man stopped by a neighbor's house to invite him. The neighbor didn't want to go and also told him, "It's not good to hunt on Sundays."

The hunter persuaded his neighbor by saying, "*No domingo também se come.* One must also eat on Sundays."

The two men crossed a small river and walked for some time through the bush without finding anything. It was as if all of the animals had disappeared. Toward the end of the afternoon, the men were frightened by some terrifying screams followed by noise and footsteps. At first, they thought it was a big man, but when it came closer, they saw that it was an animal, a black-haired, ape-like creature with a turtle's shell and one big green eye in the middle of its forehead. The men were terrified. The hunter started to shoot, but the bullets could not penetrate the beast's shell. He kept shooting, but to no avail.

The animal walked toward the hunter, grabbed him, and threw him to the ground with one of its enormous arms. The other man climbed a tree and watched in horror as the animal tore apart his friend. As it gnawed his friend's arm, it said, "*No domingo também se come.* One must also eat on Sundays." Then, gnawing a leg, it repeated, "*No domingo também se come.* One must also eat on Sundays." After the creature devoured the hunter and walked away yawning, the man who survived ran to the town and gave an account of his friend's death. Some people tried to guess what kind of an animal could have eaten the hunter. "If it has only one green eye and its feet are as big as a pestle, the creature must be the Mapinguari," said the dead hunter's cousin.

"Surely it didn't eat you, Don Luis, because you didn't have a rifle," added the others. One of the men, who knew a great deal about this sort of thing, said the hunter could have saved his life if he had shot the creature in its belly button, "because that is where its heart is." The people from the town were so outraged that they organized a search party and went hunting for the creature. They didn't have to look too hard, because the Mapinguari had come back to lick and chew on the bones of the hunter.

As soon as it saw the group of men, the beast attacked. It wanted to eat them, too. The men fired, not as their friend had done, but straight into its belly button to hit its heart. Shrieking with rage, the Mapinguari took off running and disappeared into the forest. The men gathered the uneaten bones of the hunter, put them in a sack, and took them back to town. His wife put the bones in a small coffin, and after she and her children mourned him for two nights, she took them to the cemetery. "If only he had heeded my warning," sobbed the poor widow. They say that later she took her children to Manaus where the rest of her family lived.

The Mapinguari, also known as Cape-lobo in the Pará and Maranhão regions of Brazil, is a terrifying supernatural creature with physical features similar to the cyclops of Greek mythology. Stories about this monster, considered to be one of the animal protectors in the Brazilian Amazon, also reveal the influence of Christian beliefs in the observance of the Sabbath as a day of rest. In other varieties of this tale, the Mapinguari is presented as having a foul smell, a giant mouth on its stomach, and feet pointing backward like the Curupira, another forest guardian of the Colombian and Brazilian Amazon.

Curupira: Guardian Spirit of the Forest

One day, a peasant who woke up early each morning to hunt delicious birds such as the *panguana* and *guacharaca* found a little girl with long blonde hair covering her face.

"What is this little girl doing alone in the forest? I am going to take her home to my wife," the peasant thought to himself, without realizing she was really the Curupira, the creature that guards the forest. That night, the creature returned in his dreams disguised as the little girl and said, "Man, I know you like to hunt and I am going to ask you a favor. The first animal that you see, don't shoot at it. Keep walking and you will get whatever animal you want."

In the following days, the man worked in his plot garden and forgot about the dream. But the little girl returned to talk to him in his dreams: "I know that you are going hunting soon. Please, don't forget. Don't shoot at the first animal."

The man answered in his dream: "Don't worry; I won't shoot at the first one." When he got ready to go hunting, one of his sons begged to go with him. "No, son," he told him, "I always like to go hunting alone." The son begged so hard that the man gave in. They had not been walking very long when they saw a deer by a creek. The man thought of the warning and told his son to keep going.

"But why, father? Why do we have to go so far away from home? Let's just kill this animal and get it over with!" said the son.

"No, son," said the man, not wanting to mention the dream. "We better wait for the next one." His son tried very hard to convince the man to shoot. The son insisted so much that the man fired. As soon as the animal fell, the man said, "Woe is me. Now I am going to have problems. I had a dream where I was asked not to shoot at the first animal I saw. Look, son, you insisted so much and made me fire."

"But father," said the boy, "this animal is dead. Why are you so worried?" He had hardly spoken these words when the animal got up and walked in front of them, opening his mouth and laughing as if he were human. They were shocked. Later, the man's sister and her hunting dogs came by the creek, and they told her what had occurred. The woman made fun of him and said that this would never happen to her. They were talking about this when another deer appeared, just like the first one.

Then the woman, who was a good shot, aimed and said, "Look, brother, this is how you kill one." The deer fell to the ground, but got up in front of them, laughing so much it made the dogs run away.

"Sister," said the man, "did you see? That is the Curupira that has been after me for some time. He can take any form and appear anywhere. He told me that I should not shoot at the first animal I saw. Now I am in deep trouble because I shot that animal."

When the man returned to his house, he told his wife all about it. That same night, the little girl appeared in his dream and told him, "You did not listen to my advice. You are not a man of your word."

"But my son made me do it," the man said.

"You promised me that you wouldn't shoot and you did," said the dream girl. "Now you'll see what happens to you."

A few days later, the man had to go into the forest. He saw game birds but did not shoot. He continued, and when he saw a deer, he said to himself, "Now I will do as I was told." He fired; the animal fell with the shot but in an instant got up again, laughing like a person. But the man was not afraid and repeated, "Now I am doing as I was told." He fired again, and again the animal fell and rose laughing. Time and time again the man shot; each time the animal got up.

"To make a long story short," the man would often tell his friends, "that day I shot more than twenty deer and I couldn't take even one home to my wife."

Perhaps the most talked about protector of nature in the Colombian and Brazilian Amazon, reported in Brazil since the sixteenth century, the Curupira, also known in Brazil as Mãe da Mata, and Caipora, a Tupí word meaning "forest inhabitant." He is able to take the appearance of a human or any animal in order to trick hunters and exercise his functions as a guardian of animals and plants. In the present story, as in the indigenous narratives about guardian forest spirits who appear in dreams, this hunter from Atacuari, near the border of Colombia and Peru, is advised in his sleep by the Curupira.

Chullachaki: Owner of Trees and Animals

Along the Nanay River, one of the important Amazonian rivers of Peru, there was a rubber tapper, or *shiringuero*, who worked from sunup to sundown, but the rubber trees didn't give very much latex. One morning while he was working, he saw a little fat man who had one leg smaller than the other. He was the Chullachaki, the owner of all the animals and friend of the trees.

The little man greeted the rubber tapper, "How are you doing, man?"

"Not very well," the shiringuero answered. "I have many debts."

"Well, if you want to be luckier with the rubber trees, I'll help you."

"Yes, please help me," the man begged.

The Chullachaki told him that first the man had to do him a favor and then undertake a challenge.

"Give me one of your cigars. After I smoke it, I'll fall asleep. You must kick me and hit me hard with your fists until I wake up."

The man agreed and gave him a cigar. Soon, the Chullachaki fell asleep, and the man beat him up as he had asked. When the Chullachaki awoke, he thanked the man and told him, "Well man, now let's fight. If you knock me down three times, the trees will give you more latex so that you can pay all your debts; but if it happens that I knock you down, you will die as soon as you get home."

The man thought, "This little guy can't even walk well with that short leg; if I win, I will be able to pay all my debts." They fought, and the man was able to win three times by stamping on the small foot where the Chullachaki kept all his strength.

"Now I will tell the trees to give you more latex, but don't be greedy and take so much that the trees cry," the Chullachaki said. "And if you tell anyone, you'll drop dead on the spot." He pointed out the trees the man should tap.

From then on, the rubber tapper got plenty of latex. He realized that the Chullachaki must be somebody very nice because almost every morning when he walked to work in the rubber grove, he found the Chullachaki curing animals or making the trees prettier by braiding their vines. As the time passed, the man was not only able to pay all his debts to the owner of the grove, but he was also able to buy clothes and shoes for his children so that they wouldn't go barefoot.

However, the owner of the plantation was a very greedy man. He noticed the rubber tapper's good luck, and decided to get up early to hide and to find out which rubber trees gave the most latex. Then, in order to have the same good fortune as the shiringuero, he would come in the afternoons, not with the small containers used by rubber tappers, but with great big buckets. The plantation owner made such huge gashes in the trees that the last buckets filled only with water. Some time passed. The man favored by the Chullachaki got only as much as the Chullachaki had commanded, but the owner grew rich unjustly.

One day, when the shiringuero had finished taking his share and the greedy one, lurking behind some trees, was waiting his turn, the Chullachaki appeared to both of them. He announced, "The good luck ends here." To the rubber tapper he said, "I am not going to do anything to you, but go away and don't come back." The Chullachaki turned to the rich boss and told him, "You are a man without compassion. You didn't even realize that the last buckets contained the tears of the trees instead of latex."

That afternoon, the owner became very sick with headaches and a high fever. He was so sick that he had to be taken in a canoe to the nearest post, but none of the doctors could tell him what his illness was.

The native healer who saw him could not cure him either.

The shiringuero, whose last name was Flores, is still alive; they say that because of the help he got from the Chullachaki, he never worked again. Instead, he went to Pebas, where he built a brick house.

The Chullachaki, known in the Peruvian Amazon as the owner and protector of plants and animals (similar to the Curupira, the Mãe da Seringa, and many other spirit guardians in the Amazon River basin), defends rubber trees from excessive exploitation and greed. In this story, heard from people in the Amazon River town of Pebas, the initial exchange of gifts and favors between the rubber tapper and the Chullachaki reflects the custom of reciprocity, a common relational pattern practiced in native Amazonian cultures.

Amasanga Warmi: A Ferocious Wife

*O*ne night, in one of the little villages near the Pastaza River in the Ecuadorian Amazon, it rained hard with thunder and lightning. Along with the rain fell monkeys, wild pigs (*sajinos*), turkeys, turtles, doves, and other game birds and animals that roamed in the street until the storm was over. The people of the town followed the animals into the forest, but they disappeared into some holes under the buttresses of a kapok tree. To get them out, the people threw baskets of crushed chili into the holes. Then, hundreds of *juri-juris*, which are little devil-like dogs, came out of the holes. The men began to shoot and stab at them with spears, but they escaped back into their holes.

Finally, a little girl came out of a hole; she was very pretty, with white skin and dark hair. Everyone marveled at her beauty, but when anyone tried to touch her hair, she begged them not to.

Men asked her name, and she told them it was Amasanga Warmi, which means "woman of the forest."

Since she was a person like them, the villagers took her to the town and turned her over to the priest so she could be raised Christian. After she was baptized, a family took her in and raised her until she was the right age to marry. The family said, "We will give her as a wife to the suitor who brings ten turkeys and ten monkeys to show he is responsible." Three men came to ask for her hand, but only one of them was responsible enough to bring the ten turkeys and the ten monkeys, proving he would be able to support her and any children she might have.

After the wedding, the man took her to his home in the woods. On the way, the woman promised to be faithful and to be a good wife, but told her husband that he should never touch her head, even to caress her hair. The man vowed to respect her wish, and as she had promised, the woman took very good care of the house and her husband by bringing him the best fruit and food from the garden. In the rainy season, as people liked to do in Pastaza, she would pick the lice from her husband's hair while singing and longing for sunny days. But each time her husband wanted to groom the lice out of her hair, she reminded him that he had promised never to touch it.

Although they were happy together, the husband often thought to himself, "Why doesn't she allow me to touch her head?"

One day, the man was overcome with curiosity to find out what was in his wife's hair, and decided to investigate. When his wife went to bring *yuca*, or manioc roots, from the garden, he told her, "Woman, I am going hunting. I will be back later," and left ahead of her. He went close to the garden and hid himself beside the trail where the woman would be walking. When she had dug out the yuca, cut the *palmitos* (hearts of palm), and had started walking back to the house, the man jumped out from behind her. He grabbed her and messed up the hair on the back of her head. So doing, he discovered her other face, which was like that of the juri-juris—the little devil-like dogs—who hide under the kapok trees.

His wife looked at him with sadness and said, "Why have you shamed me, discovering my face that is not meant to live in this world but only under the kapok trees? You are my husband and I have never wanted to harm you. I have worked hard in the garden, bringing fruit and making good *masato* [manioc beer] for the household." Then the woman, who had claimed to be Amasanga Warmi, looked at him with her diabolic juri-juri face and shrieked with evil laughter, showing her razor-sharp teeth. She grabbed her husband with her animal grip and opened his skull to eat his brains, the part she liked most. Afterward, she ate his heart and then went back under the kapok trees.

Descendents of the Shuar indigenous groups, who live in the small town of Tena, Ecuador, and have adopted Christian beliefs, tell different versions of this story. Apparent in this tale is the clear influence of indigenous myths with fierce creatures capable of taking human form. The story portrays the spirit's nature illustrated by the woman's refusal to have her identity revealed and the murder of her husband.

A fisherman and his two sons gut their catch in Santa Sofía,
a town on the banks of the Amazon in Colombia
at the Peruvian border.

A maid in a small hotel in Lethen, Guyana, taking a break to relate one of her tales about Kanaima.

A shaman from the Ecuadorian Amazon, near the Napo River, performs his daily chores. When he is not advising people or treating them for illness, he goes to the forest to collect medicinal and psychoactive plants and to gather wood.

Passing down an oral tradition, an elderly man who has moved from the forest to town tells stories to his granddaughter, who goes to elementary school in Riberalta, Bolivia.

Natives from a variety of ethnic groups near Leticia,
Colombia, tell stories at night while chewing coca leaves
and visiting with neighbors.

A group of women in Centro Arenal, Peru,
tell stories while washing clothes.

A boat captain and his wife, who are Cocama descendants on the Nanay River in Peru. While their children are tending the fishing nets nearby and selling food at the port, he and his wife transport passengers to local communities.

This experienced hunter, a descendant of indigenous Cocama natives in the upper Amazon, now is a shaman in the community of San Rafael, near Iquitos, Peru. In this picture, he tells his experiences in the forest.

A Shaman storyteller mashes ayahuasca vine before boiling
it for use at a ceremony near the Itaya River
in the Peruvian Amazon.

Ayahuasca, a magic potion used by shamans for
communication with water and forest spirits.

A fisherman from the island of Marajó, at the mouth of the Amazon River, where it meets the Atlantic Ocean. He prepares his catch for sale at the market.

A mechanic, who in his youth was a rubber tapper in the area near the Yavari River, tells stories of fantastic creatures that scared him in the forest.

A hunter, who once was a logger in the area near the
Putumayo River, finds a moment to tell stories while taking
a break in his plot garden. On the left, the author.

Children observe their grandfather making a canoe in their backyard.

A flute, drums, and rattles made from gourds are all forest
dwellers needed to animate a gathering.

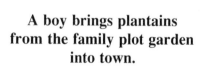

A boy brings plantains
from the family plot garden
into town.

The ever-present Amazonian pink dolphin.

Pulling up manioc (*Manihot esculenta*) for their daily meals.

Amazonian wood to be exported in the global market.

A bush of toé (*Brugmansia suaveolens*), a divinatory plant.

A local from Iquitos, Peru, preparing to appear as the Chullachaki, the spirit defender of the forest.

The old Hotel Palace of Iquitos built by a wealthy rubber baron during the rubber boom era.

A hunter returns from the deep forest with his catch.

A passenger boat makes many stops to take riverine and forest dwellers and their products to Amazonian towns and cities.

An Amazonian boy and his favorite pet.

It is possi-
ble to swim
right out-
side your
door during
the rainy
season.

Life during the rainy season.

Tucunaré is always a precious catch.

Learning from community elders.

Epereji: Animal Guardian

*I*n Conquista, one of the villages on the Madre de Dios River, there was a man who made his living hunting and selling game to rubber collectors. The hunting wasn't very good, and one day he was hiding by a watering hole. Just as he had a few small deer, or *guazos* as they are called in the Bolivian Amazon, within range, he heard the sound of a horn, and the animals disappeared as if they were called away.

His wife scolded him for coming home empty-handed; she complained that he could not even feed his own family. The man returned to the watering hole. He saw an *anta*, or tapir, coming and was able to kill it with a single shot. He was preparing to carry the animal away when he saw a little man less than half a meter tall coming down from a tree. The hunter became quiet. The little man was very furry and wore a straw hat. He went up to the tapir and gave it two slaps in the face. The animal came back to life as if nothing had happened.

The little man said, "I am the Epereji, the guide and caretaker of the animals. I know you have problems with your wife, and I'd like to help you." He gave the hunter a small ox horn and told him, "This will attract the animals, but kill sparingly and do not tell anyone." Then the Epereji rode off on the revived tapir.

Right away, the hunter attracted a delicious rodent known as *jochi pintado* with the horn; he killed it and happily took it to his wife. From then on, when in need, all he had to do was sound the horn and various animals would come and he could kill them easily.

Time passed, and the man told his wife about his good fortune and showed her the ox horn that the Epereji had given him that he now kept under their bed. The woman was very happy. One day when her husband was not home, she loaned the horn to her greedy brother. Wanting to salt and sell lots of meat, her brother went to the watering hole and killed and wounded almost all the deer, the jochis pintados, and any other animals that came to drink.

After a few days, the hunter decided to go hunting again, but he could not find the horn. "Who took the horn?" he asked his wife. She swore that she had put it back beneath the bed after her brother had returned it. They searched in vain. There was no food, so the hunter told his wife he would go hunting again and that he would not come back until he got another horn and brought more meat.

Once more, he hid by the watering hole. Several tapirs arrived. He shot the biggest one, which fell to the ground. When he tried to retrieve it, the animal got up. He fired again but the animal came running at him.

He didn't know what happened next—he blacked out.

When he came to, he saw the Epereji riding on the tapir that he had shot. After asking for forgiveness, the man begged for the use of the horn again, but the Epereji told the hunter that since his brother-in-law had slaughtered and wounded so many animals, he had been working to cure them from the harm committed by the greedy man. The Epereji said, "I told you not to tell anyone. So now I won't lend it to you."

This is what happened, and the man had to go home crying to his wife.

This story, told in the vicinities of Conquista in the Bolivian Amazon, speaks of the ability of the forest guardians to transform themselves into the animals they protect. In this tale, the Epereji shifts from his original appearance in the form of a little man to that of a wounded animal to attack the hunter and then return to his original shape. As he serves as caretaker of the forest, the Epereji shares many characteristics with other supernatural defenders such as the Sacharuna and Huagrachaqui from Ecuador; the Salvaje from Venezuela; the Chullachaki, Yashingu, and Shapushico from Peru; the Curupira from Colombia and Brazil; and the Cabokinha, Mapinguari, and Mãe da Seringa from Brazil.

Curupira's Son

A man came with his wife to live in the forest. The settlers and natives who lived there told them to take the land they needed to feed themselves. The man said to his wife, "This land looks good, and these people don't know how to take advantage of it. Let's take all we can."

When the neighbors saw that he was clearing a great deal of forest, they asked, "Are you bringing more family to live with you?"

"No," the man said, "I'm going to plant a lot and save for the future."

Time passed. One nice day, the man went out hunting, and a very pretty girl appeared in his path. She offered to take him to a place where there were many animals. The man accepted her offer, and he was easily able to kill an armadillo. When he arrived home, his wife was very happy. But her happiness was short-lived. By the time she finished cooking the animal, the meat had disappeared and only a few burnt bones were left.

The man ran into the girl again the next time he went hunting. This time she asked, "Are you bringing more family to live with you?"

"No," he said, "I'm clearing the land to plant corn and rice to save for the future." She once again led him to a place where there were many small edible rodents called *borugas*; and the man was able to kill one easily. His wife was happy, but this time she wasn't going to let the same thing occur that had happened to the armadillo. She kept a lid on the pot, and never left the kitchen.

In spite of the woman's efforts, the meat disappeared after being cooked.

The man went hunting and ran into the girl again. Even though he was afraid she was playing tricks on him, he didn't care because she was so pretty. While he chatted with the girl, his wife was visited by a new neighbor who came to introduce himself. The woman was grateful for his visit and offered him some manioc beer.

After talking with the woman for a while, the neighbor said, "I think it would be best for me to spend the night with you. I don't think your husband will be home this evening."

Alarmed, the good woman asked why.

The man answered, "Your husband is spending the night with a girl he met in the woods, so the best thing is for me to keep you company."

Sure enough, night fell and her husband did not come home. The next day, he returned. He told his wife he had gotten lost.

A few months passed. The man had managed to clear a large piece of land, and his wife was going to have their first child. One day, while the man was pulling up yuca, a very handsome stranger showed up where he was working and said, "Neighbor, you must drop what you're doing and run to your wife. At this very moment, she is giving birth to our child."

"What did you say?" asked the surprised man.

The stranger answered, "That's right—she is giving birth to my son. Maybe you don't remember. The night you spent with the girl in the forest, I spent with your wife in your house."

The man tried to avenge himself by throwing his shovel at the stranger's chest, but his efforts were in vain. The stranger disappeared.

The man ran home to find his wife had just given birth, but oddly, the baby was nowhere to be seen. She and the midwife told him that the minute after it was born, the child, who had one foot pointing backward, had run out and climbed a *guama* tree. Desperate, the poor man got a ladder to climb the tree and bring down the child. That very instant, the stranger, accompanied by the girl from the forest, appeared out of nowhere and shook the ladder until he fell. Lying on the ground, the man saw the child descend from the tree and run away with the girl and the stranger. As they left, the girl said to the man, "We will take the boy. We need him to help us take care of the forest." As they got further and further away, the man realized the strangers must be the child's parents. They each had a foot pointing backward.

The Curupira is known as the powerful master of animals with metamorphic features. There are stories where he presents himself as an attractive person, a friend, or a family member of his victim in order to take him or her to live in enchanted places. Sometimes, he only wants to punish a hunter, causing him to become lost in the thick forest. His actions against mestizo inhabitants who destroy the rain forest reflect the ecological thought of indigenous Amazonians.

Seringa: Mother of the Rubber Trees

*T*here was a man in the Brazilian Amazon who lived alone on the riverbanks of the Yavari River and tapped rubber trees. While he worked, he repeated in a sad voice, "Woe is me, my life is so hard. I spend it working and have no one to help me. When I return home, I must cook my own supper alone." So it went until one day he arrived home from a day's labor to find a surprise. Served on the table was a piece of tapir smoked with *farinha* (manioc flour), and other things that he had left ready to cook for supper. The embers of the fire were still hot. The man marveled and ate the meal happily, but he could not overcome his curiosity and kept asking himself who could have done this.

The next day after breakfast, he followed his usual habit of leaving a piece of salted fish, beans, plantains, and farinha ready to prepare for his evening meal when he returned. While working, he thought contentedly about the food he had set aside for his supper. When he arrived home, he found the same delightful surprise. The fish had been simmered with plantains and manioc, and was served with farinha and a jug of water. Beside the plates on the table, someone had carved an inscription with a knife: "Humans don't know what trees know."

This time, the rubber tapper felt fear as well as satisfaction and curiosity. He said to himself, "This is very strange. I'm going to find out who wrote this!" The next day, he decided to return home a bit earlier than usual. He wanted to hide in the house, but it was so small that he had to conceal himself behind a nearby *castanheira* (Brazilian nut tree). After a short wait, he saw a young woman step out of a *seringa*, or rubber tree, that grew very close to the house. She had golden hair and her clothes were made of bark.

Astonished, the man watched as the woman stretched her arms to wake herself up, as if she had been asleep for a very long time. She went into the house and began to make a fire. Instead of using a feather fan to encourage the fire, the girl whistled, and in an instant, a bird flew to her. She held the bird by its legs near the flames so that it could flap its wings to fan the fire. When the fire was ready, she let go and the bird flew into some nearby bushes. All the while, she kept glancing in the direction of the rubber

---

tapper's hiding place, as if she suspected his presence. Finally, the man couldn't stand it any longer and decided to reveal himself.

When she saw him, the girl fled, passing through the walls as if they were made of air.

The man ran into the house, and saw that nothing had changed. In the fireplace were ashes from the day before. He was very sad, for now his life returned to what it had been before.

The girl never came back to his house, but she appeared in a dream and said to him, "Why couldn't you be happy just with my help? Now I won't help you with anything ever again!" These words proved true. He never again returned home to find his food already cooked, and the trees that had been so generous gave him less and less latex each day. The man was forced to leave the forest and go to live in one of the villages built by new settlers prospecting for gold. He searched for a means of support and found work selling popsicles and sweets to people at the port.

Indigenous stories of the Amazon establish that trees, animals, lakes, rivers, and other natural elements have mothers who protect them. They also grant permission for people to enter the forest and help them in their daily lives. Variations of the present story, from the mouths of rubber tappers from the Yavari River and many other places in the Brazilian Amazon, describe the Mãe da Seringa, or the mother of the rubber trees, with a cut in her arms similar to those made by tappers on rubber trees.

The Flute of the Chullachaki

A man and his two brothers had been hunting for a few days without finding any animals. Discouraged and hungry, his brothers returned home. But the man stayed behind to hunt for something to take to his family. The next day, he found a few sajinos and followed them until he saw them disappear into the entrance to a cave. He went inside and found himself in the middle of a grove of fruit trees that shaded a cleared area covered with leaves. Sitting under a tree loaded with small yellow fruits known as *caimito* was a man who seemed to be a dwarf. He was grandfather Chullachaki, the spirit of the forest who, according to the elders, had one leg that was smaller than the other and who could turn into a person, into a relative, or slip into the skin of any animal and become one of them, maybe a monkey, a tapir, or a bird.

Since the Chullachaki could read people's minds, he realized that the man was hungry and he told him he could help. He picked up a *nacanaca*, a coral snake, and as soon as it was in his hands, it turned into a beautiful *pifuano*, a flute used by forest dwellers. "This pifuano produces music that only animals can hear and it makes them come to you. But if you don't use it well, you will be punished," grandfather Chullachaki told the man. "Keep it in this sack that I am giving you and only use it when your family needs meat to eat." Later, the spirit told him that if he liked, he could help himself to the fruits in his chacra, or forest plot garden.

While the hunter was eating the furry-skinned *zapote* fruit and *guabas*, elongated seedy fruits covered with juicy cotton-like flesh, he saw a woman and some children coming close to the trees as if to take the fruits. But they only smelled them. "Those must be the Chullachaki's relatives," thought the man, noticing they all had one leg smaller than the other. He also realized that none of them had buttocks. The man thanked the Chullachaki and left the plot garden the same way he had come in. In the path toward his house, he began to chuckle to himself: "Ha, ha, ha, Chullachakis don't have buttocks. Ha, ha, ha, Chullachakis don't have buttocks."

Further along, he played the flute and was able to hunt down a wild pig.

When he got to the village, everyone was so surprised that even the dogs and a macaw celebrated. His brothers and sisters and other family members came to the

---

celebration to drink manioc beer and eat. The man told his story about the Chullachakis that only smelled the fruits and who had no buttocks. "Ha, ha, ha, Chullachakis don't have buttocks. Ha, ha, ha, Chullachakis don't have buttocks, that is really funny," laughed all the men, women, and children. "Ha, ha, ha, Chullachakis don't have buttocks."

"Ha, ha, ha, Chullachakis don't have buttocks," the male macaw who lived in the family kitchen repeated over and over that night.

That night, everyone drank masato, and one of the man's brothers said, "What we need is to play that flute that only animals can hear to get so much meat that we can fill this kitchen to the roof and overcome our poverty."

"That way we won't have to spend so many days looking for animals all over the forest," added the oldest brother. Then the man who had hunted the sajino said that was not possible because he had promised the Chullachaki he would hunt with it only when his family was in need.

His brothers told him he was a fool, but the man still refused.

After that, the man did not have to go very far to hunt animals. He would play melodies that attracted the animals and then choose only those he wanted. His brothers came over very frequently to try to convince him to use the flute. "Brother, if we could only use the flute to hunt animals, our families would be better off than any family around here."

Once again, the younger brother told them that he could not do this because grandfather Chullachaki would get angry.

His brothers came many times to ask him to loan them the flute. One day while they were drinking too much, the younger brother gave in to their begging. They all went to the forest with big bags and salt, and brought their friends to help them bring home delicious game birds like *panguanas* and meat from wild pigs and tapirs or any other meat they could hunt to sell in the Belen market in Iquitos. As for the flute, they carried it in the same sack that the Chullachaki had put it in. Whenever they got to where they thought the animals were, the greediest brother said, "Brother, here is where we can call the animals to be hunted. Let me be the one who plays the music only animals can hear on the flute." The man raised the flute to his mouth, and at the moment it sounded, it turned into a coral snake and bit him in the face, killing him.

The brothers went home, disheartened. The next morning, the hunter who had received the flute from the Chullachaki died suddenly as he ate breakfast.

Family members recount that the macaw laughed all day long in the kitchen, "Ha, ha, ha, Chullachakis don't have buttocks. Ha, ha, ha, Chullachakis don't have buttocks."

Many stories of the Chullachaki describe his home as a place similar to the small chacras or plot gardens that Amazonian people have in the forest. According to storytellers, this is where he takes animals injured by hunters to cure them. This tale reveals the familiarity between forest inhabitants and the spirits, as the hunter refers to the Chullachaki as "grandfather." Such familiarity is inherited from the indigenous Amazonian vision that believes in a cosmic kinship between humans and all other physical or non-material beings.

The Hunter and the Curupira

*O*n the banks of the Iça River in the Brazilian Amazon there once lived a very skilled hunter. One day when he was coming home with a *mutum*, or turkey-sized bird, and a few small monkeys, he lay down to rest at the foot of a tree. He slept there until dusk, when he was awakened by the noise of something pounding the tree. When he saw its hairy face and one of its feet pointing backward, he realized it was the Curupira, the guardian of the forest. The man stayed very still, and the Curupira sat down beside him.

A few hours later, the Curupira said, "Give me a piece of your arm to eat."

The hunter, who until then thought that the Curupira was friendly, was worried. "I can't just let him eat me like this," he thought. So he cut off the arm of one of the monkeys he had killed and handed it over.

The Curupira swallowed it and stayed right by his side. Later, the Curupira said, "Give me your heart to eat."

The hunter slashed through the chest of the dead monkey and handed over the heart.

The Curupira ate it with pleasure but then said, "Man, I asked for your heart and you gave me the heart of a dead monkey. Hand me a knife so I can get yours out of your ribs."

The man acted as if he were going to give the knife to him, but when the Curupira reached to get it, the man drove it into his chest.

In the morning, the hunter discovered that the Curupira's body had turned into a tree trunk.

The hunter returned to his house and told his wife that he wanted to go back to see what kind of wood it was. The two of them went into the forest to find it. When they saw it, they realized that it had turned hard as stone. They tried to carry it, but it was too heavy. The man told his wife that they should try to find out what was inside. He was not able to cut it with his machete, so his wife went back to the house and got the best ax they had.

The man hit the trunk with such force that sparks flew off.

After he had hacked at it for a long time, the Curupira came out of the trunk and said, "Well, I am very grateful to you, man, because if you hadn't hit me so hard, I never would have woken up!"

Even though in his role as forest guardian the Curupira acts as a vindictive creature who punishes those who abuse nature, there are many stories where he appears as a fun-loving spirit who plays jokes on people. It is said that this guardian spirit, whose shape varies from one region to another, has the habit of beating on the base of the samaumeira tree (Ceiba pentandra) and other giant trees to bring rain, and that he causes mysterious sounds in the forest.

The Hunter and the Curupira

Yanapuma: Black Jaguar Vampire

*T*here once was a *mitayero*, or hunter, who was hired to kill tapirs, wild pigs, monkeys, and other animals to feed some loggers near the Pachitea River. One day, as the mitayero and the camp's cook searched for the next day's meal, they saw a strange white animal that looked like a calf. "Look, there's a young cow," said the cook, "I wonder how it got here."

"That's not a cow, that's a Yanapuma, the devil's jaguar," replied the hunter. "We'd better go back to camp and tell everyone about this, so that we can move the camp to a place far away."

The cook laughed at him for believing such nonsense. Still, they hurried back to the camp and told everyone what had happened. The woodcutters didn't believe the story either. The mitayero told them, "This white jaguar is harmless during the day, but at night, he turns into a ferocious black killer who will attack the camp. His body becomes possessed by the devil and no bullet can harm him. The only way to kill him is with a spear."

A few of the loggers made fun of him. "We will see what harm he can do when he faces our bullets," said one of the men.

"We can't afford to run away from the cedar and mahogany trees here just because of these ridiculous stories," said another.

The next day, the hunter went alone to get some food. He killed an edible monkey, or *maquisapa*, and at sunset he returned happily to camp with his catch. But when he got there, he discovered the dead bodies of his friends strewn on the ground, with their fired rifles beside them. He examined the corpses, which were unharmed except for marks on their necks. "This has been the work of the Yanapuma," he thought. The marks were small holes the Yanapuma made with his teeth as he sucked their blood.

At first the man was overcome by sorrow, but then he became furious. Thinking that the Yanapuma might still be close by, he climbed a tree and waited with his spear. At midnight, he heard the Yanapuma's roar. When he smelled the man, the beast started to climb the tree. The mitayero was frightened but took heart and was able to stab the animal with his spear.

With a terrifying yelp, the Yanapuma fell down beneath the tree.

The mitayero thought, "The female Yanapuma will come to look for her mate. I better wait." A short time later, another beast appeared. She saw her dead partner, moaned, and then became so furious that she tried to climb the tree to avenge her companion. But the man was prepared for the attack and was able to kill her, too.

After watching her die, the man came down from the tree and continued mourning his friends. He wanted to bury them at sunrise, but first he had to tell their relatives at another camp, three days away. Since it was such a long trip, he decided to begin his journey in the middle of the night. On the way, he heard the voices of his friends who had died under the Yanapuma's fangs calling to him from another place, "Friend, friend, forgive us for laughing at you. Forgive us and tell everyone you meet what happened here."

Other stories about this black jaguar present it as a creature who lives in the water and who is capable of hypnotizing his victims. According to some Amazonians, the existence of these animals in one area of the forest can be verified by shamans who ingest sacred forest plants such as ayahuasca (Banisteriopsis caapi) *and toé* (Brugmansia suaveolens). *These plants make it possible for them to see the future and consult with the spirit "owners" of the forest.*

CHAPTER 5

Tales of Dark and Malevolent Shamans

Kanaima: Dark Shamans

*J*n Lethen, Guyana, there lived an adventurous boy named Paul. One day when his parents were not at home, some people who looked like his neighbors came to his door and invited him to go fishing. On the way, the supposed neighbors were all drinking from gourds and their faces changed to look like monkeys, turning small and red. Then the oldest man grabbed Paul's hand and said, "We are Kanaima and we are not going fishing. We are going to a party down the river where there will be a lot of *cassiri* (manioc beer) to drink and barbecue to eat until we're stuffed. You are coming. Don't try to escape. If you don't do as we say, we will kill you right here."

"Please don't kill me. I will do what you say," pleaded the boy.

"Very well," said the chief.

They arrived at a house on the river where there lived a fat, blond lady and her husband who were always trying to protect their dwelling from the bad spirits in the forest. On the banks, the Kanaima, or violent sorcerers, sniffed a leaf and changed from monkeys into the fat lady's neighbors. They mashed some manioc to make more beer and built a fire. Then they made the boy sniff the leaf and sent him to invite the fat lady to come and celebrate with them.

Paul knocked on the door and told her that he came on behalf of her neighbors to invite her to the party. The woman went down to the river, but she realized that these were not her neighbors. According to her husband, they were Kanaima, people with monkey faces who would appear in the rainy season and walk around in the forest transforming themselves into whatever they wanted. The woman tried to run to her house, but before she could get there, the Kanaima beat her to death with sticks. After, they cut her heart into small pieces and put the pieces in their pockets. Then they cut her body into good-sized chunks and barbecued her. Later, Paul opened the fat lady's door for them. The parts of her that they had not eaten they took inside the house and placed in the pot where the man and woman kept beer. While they were drinking cassiri and seasoning the woman's meat with herbs, they entertained themselves by taking out the pieces of her heart from their pockets to smell—everybody liked it. They offered some to Paul, but he said, "No, I don't want any. With all due respect, I didn't know you were inviting me to this kind of barbecue."

The Kanaima laughed and told him that if he did not like it, to stay outside and warn them when the woman's husband was coming. Before anyone could enter the house, the Kanaima hid the pot of meat under the floor and turned into ants.

When the husband arrived, there were ants all over the house. The man said, "What are all these ants doing in the house?" Nobody answered. The man swept them out and went to the river to look for his wife. Then the Kanaima turned into black flies that flew into the house, happily smelling the woman's meat. They ate what they could and then fell asleep on the furniture and the walls. At that moment, the woman's father showed up to borrow some tools, and before he left he smoked out the black flies. Thrown outside once again, the Kanaima turned into cows, pigs, ducks, sheep, and other animals that the couple kept. They went under the tree where Paul had fallen asleep and made noise to wake him up. When he asked them to let him go home, the chief of the Kanaima came out of the hog's grunt and said, "Boy, get up. We are going to another party."

Paul tried to run but the Kanaima stopped him by trampling on him.

The chief said to him, "We told you we were Kanaima. We come from the mountains to the forest and we can turn into any kind of animal or plant. If we want to eat you, we will eat you."

The boy cried, "Please sir, please don't eat me. You have already had your barbecue. Let me go home."

But the Kanaima would not let him go. They took him through the forest and the plains, where they kept having drunken cassiri beer parties and harming more and more people.

When the rains stopped, they finally let Paul go free. It was only then that he was able to return home to tell everyone how wonderful the Kanaima felt when they were drunk on cassiri and full of people-meat. His parents were pleased to have him back. Paul began hunting and fishing with his friends like he used to.

The next year, however, when the rains came, he was home alone when he saw some people coming who had red monkey faces. They knocked at the door and Paul answered.

They introduced themselves as his neighbors and once again invited him to go with them to a party.

Stories about Kanaima, who practice attack sorcery, are very common among the Amazonian people from Guyana and Venezuela. This tale and its variations, obtained in Lethen, Guyana, reflect the way European colonizers evaluated indigenous practices of

the ingestion of fermented products derived from manioc and the use of visionary plants able to provide a bridge between this world and that of the spirits. The association that newcomers made of indigenous groups and their descendents with cannibalism and violence was used as justification for an imposed colonial order and evangelism in northeastern Amazonia.

The Spirits of the Stones: Evil Spirits

*O*ne day, a peasant who lived on the banks of the Madre de Dios River in the Bolivian Amazon said to his parents, "I don't want to work the land anymore. I am going to learn sorcery." His father was not happy about it, but gave his blessing and wished his son good luck.

The man went down the river looking for a master of the art of sorcery. Finally, in the town of Cobija, he found a sorcerer who did magic by blowing on stones that he carried around in a black bag. According to the master, in these stones there lived some spirits that had the power of healing and that gave help in matters of love and business. The man stayed with his teacher for a while, and then went to work with the stones on his own.

In exchange for serving him in his sorcery, the spirits in the stones asked him to protect them from the sun by putting them in bags made of black fabric. They warned that if he didn't, they would kill him. They also told the man that during storms, he should put them on the big rock in the backyard. Under this arrangement, everything went well, and the man was able to live by his art. But many times it happened that the man was not able to solve his cases or help people suffering from mortal illnesses.

He tried to find his master but could not.

However, the spirits guessed what he wanted and in his bag there appeared other stones that had the ability to cure deadly diseases, and even kill, according to what they said. "We want to stay with you. We are going to give you power over life and death, but you must obey us." The man agreed and was able to save his patients and help people with their businesses. His reputation spread far and wide and people sought help all along the Madre de Dios river, from Pando and even Brazil. His skill made him rich. The only thing he had to do was guard the stones from the sun and satisfy the demand of the spirits during storms and lightning.

His father was happy to see his prosperity, but he was a Christian and suspicious of magic. Worried, he asked his son, "Couldn't it be that you are working with something evil?"

But his son avoided the subject by saying, "I'm rich. I can buy anything I want."

One day, the spirits of the stones demanded that he kill a certain number of people. "If you don't do it," the stones said, "we'll stop helping you and kill you, too."

At first, the man did not want to obey, but he did not want to risk losing his help or his life and agreed to comply. He decided to make clay models of just those people who were his enemies and with the power that the spirits gave him he killed them. He believed that this would please the spirits, but it didn't. They appeared in his dreams and told him to increase the number of victims.

The man did not want to obey and told the spirits, "I can't keep killing for no reason."

When they heard this, the rancorous spirits caused a motorcycle taxi to run him over. For a month he was almost dead. In order to survive, the man agreed to keep killing.

During this time, however, the people in the town began to suspect that his sorcery had something to do with all the sudden deaths. A priest advised them against the man; and they almost burned him alive in his house. Feeling cornered, he went to his father and confessed everything.

"The spirits that live in the stones come to me at night and tell me to kill people," he said. He described making clay models of his victims and stabbing them in the heart, sometimes as many as six a month. "If I don't do it, father, the owners of the stones will come and kill me. What am I going to do?"

His father replied, "Well, son, this is the devil; he sends these spirits to do harm to people. That's his mission in the world, but I have an acquaintance who knows something about magic. I'll ask him for help."

This man advised them to take the stones out of their sack and put them in the roots of an almond tree where no light could get to them and where they would be peaceful. That's what they did.

Time passed. One day when the man and his father were walking by the place where they had left the stones, they saw that the tree had been burned. Its trunk had been shattered as if all the bolts of lightning had struck it. The man's father said, "You see? I was right. Look how these evil things repaid the almond tree, killing the tree that was serving them so well.

This is one of many stories told by those who work carrying merchandise in wooden carts in the streets and as vendors in outdoor markets in Riberalta, Bolivia. The

actions of the young shaman, which are destined to cause harm to people, are part of the negative use of what is called "sympathetic magic" that some Amazonian shamans employ. This practice, which goes back to antiquity in most cultural traditions of the world, is based on the notion that actions against the objects that represent a person can produce the same effect on the person even if he or she is far away.

Pact with the Devil

*J*n the region of Beni, in the Bolivian Amazon, there lived a man who wanted to be rich. One day, he went to a sorcerer and told him that he would do anything if he could be wealthy. The sorcerer took him to a hut on one of the islands of the Beni River, where they met the devil, who was dressed in a cape and carried a black brief-case. The ambitious man proposed to give him his soul in exchange for riches.

The devil agreed, but warned him, "One day when you least expect it, I will come for your soul."

They arranged the matter, and soon thereafter the man began to have good fortune.

He claimed part of the forest for himself, and in that region he not only dominated the native people (whom he unjustly called barbarians), but also he took advantage of the settlers who came there to live. So that his plantations and villages would produce more, he brought in foreign administrators who helped him with efficiency. The workers obeyed him, producing bales of rubber of the very best quality, and gathering fine furs, quinine bark, and nuts, with which they filled the cargo boats that came from the Orthon River, the Madre de Dios River, the Mamoré, and others. Later, his merchandise left in steamboats from Beni to the Amazon and from there went by sea to other countries. The boats came back with chests full of silver, canned foods, perfumes, liquors, and the finest clothing for the managers and friends of the house.

For them, and for his own entertainment, the man had a theater built where he brought dancers, opera singers, and movie stars to his world in the forest. They said he was very generous to his friends and the workers who served him well, but he would use manacles, iron rings, to secure the hands of lazy people to the ground, and kill his enemies. He had so much power that the government of his country listened to what he said from his house in Beni. When he found out that the government was building a railway along a route that was not convenient for him, he advised the president to have the work stopped. Later, he had the abandoned rails picked up so he could use them in the construction of his villages.

This went on for many years. But one day when he was resting peacefully in his home after lunch, the sky suddenly became very dark as if a great fog were about to descend, and an immense storm shook his house. There was lightning and thunder, but no rain. In the middle of this dry storm, a man dressed very elegantly with a cape and a top hat arrived at his house. He rang the doorbell and entered the office of the rich man.

From the office, his family heard loud voices, along with loud bangs, like fists pounding on the man's desk. His wife and his daughter, who were knitting peacefully on the terrace and had seen the visitor coming, were afraid for the stranger's life.

When the visitor came out of the office, thunder rumbled and the smell of sulfur lingered.

The storm disappeared and the sunny day returned. His wife and daughter ran inside and found the man in despair. When they asked him what had happened, he answered, "Now my hour has come. That was my master who has come for me."

In the months that followed, the man did not lose his strength. On the contrary, his demands doubled on the workers to increase his wealth, and the overseers who were not severe enough learned personally about the whips and manacles he kept. He ordered two other beautiful houses built, one for his daughter and another for his wife. It is believed that the man also had many hiding places built in the giant river rocks and in the walls of his house (no one knows where for sure) to put the bags of silver, jewels, and other treasures he had accumulated.

But no kingdom or person can last forever. A year after the visit, the man got a stomachache while he was eating pork. He became so ill that not even the foreign doctors that he had at his side were able to save him. That night he died. His body lay in state so that his relatives could come to pay their respects. His death was so important that the president sent his own guard to fire a salute of honor.

On the morning that they were going to bury him, his body was not in the casket.

His wife and children had to fill his coffin with rocks from the Beni River to fake it. The workers believed that the devil had wanted to take the body of the man straight to hell. "But those were lies," Don Julio Rada used to say. "Because the devil is only interested in souls, he does not need to take anybody's body."

This tale, well-known from Riberalta to Guayaramerín in the Bolivian Amazon, tells of someone who sells his soul to the devil as in Goethe's Faust. *The story takes place in the era of the rubber boom when the exportation of this "white gold" from Amazonian trees to the United States and Europe brought great riches and power to a few entrepreneurs. According to storytellers, such was the case of Nicolás Suárez, owner of the Suárez House, whose headquarters were situated on the Beni River in Bolivia.*

Dañero: Malicious Sorcerer

*N*ear San Fernando de Atabapo, in the Venezuelan Amazon, there lived a girl who had two suitors—one who worked very hard on a small farm collecting *castaña*, or Brazilian nuts, and one who was very lazy. Since the girl's parents did not like the lazy one, they tried to keep her away from him because he didn't bring her fruit or other food from his farm.

During this time, at night, at the girl's house and at the neighboring farms, everyone began hearing a whistling sound, "Píííí Matí Chupirííí Jííí, Píííí Matí Chupirííí Jííí." This is the sound that a Dañero, or evil sorcerer, makes with a little frog bone to announce that he is going to harm someone. In the evenings, people started to close and lock their doors. The dogs barked at the Dañero but came back shivering in fright from the scent of the jaguar oil that Dañeros wear.

The girl's father, who was suspicious of the lazy suitor, found out that he belonged to a family of Dañeros, who use the knowledge of the native people to harm people with *curare*, a poison from plants able to cause paralysis, and potions that work both nearby and from far away. According to the old ones, "They paint themselves with coloring from shrubs and go out naked to whistle at night before doing evil."

Following the Dañero's whistles, the hardworking suitor became sick and died, and the whistles stopped. But a short time later, the whistles "Píííí Matí Chupirííí Jííí, Píííí Matí Chupirííí Jííí" returned, every night closer and closer to the girl's house. Her father went to the landowner to ask for his help.

The landowner was a very determined man and said he did not believe that the Dañeros were invincible; in fact, they were no different from anyone else. He said he was going to scare the Dañero away with gunfire. He got his workers to set up their rifles with strings attached to their triggers so that they would fire into the air if anyone tripped the cords.

The workers said, "Whether the whistler is a Dañero or just an obnoxious human, we're going to scare him away."

The whistling returned, "Píííí Matí Chupirííí Jííí, Píííí Matí Chupirííí Jííí," and the guns went off.

The men ran and with their flashlights they made out the face of the Dañero, which was painted with *onoto,* a red or yellowish-red dye obtained from seeds, so that nobody would recognize him. They screamed at him, "Get the hell away from here and don't ever come back!"

The Dañero vanished, leaving behind the heavy stench of jaguar oil.

Several days passed, and then the whistling "Píííí Matí Chupirííí Jííí, Píííí Matí Chupirííí Jííí" continued at night, each time closer to the girl's house. She went to the landowner and said that the best thing to do would be to kill the Dañero.

The workers were happy to oblige and prepared their rifles.

When the Dañero returned, whistling, "Píííí Matí Chupirííí Jííí, Píííí Matí Chupirííí Jííí," he tripped on the cords and the bullets penetrated his chest. To find out who he was, the men tracked him by the trail of blood he left behind. They heard him fall into the river. But they couldn't see his face. They only saw how he cut out his guts with a knife to feed to the voracious fish. Then he dove under the water so that none would know his fate; he could survive in the other world of the Dañeros.

The girl and her family now live in Puerto Ayacucho, and her mother says, "That's the way they do it. That way we don't think they can die."

Stories about Dañeros, whose violent sorcery is similar to the Kanaima from Guyana, are heard among storytellers from the riverine towns of San Fernando de Atabapo and Puerto Ayacucho in the Venezuelan Amazon. Dañeros are accused of being evil shamans who use the ancient knowledge from Arawak indigenous groups about medicinal plants and poisons to commit crimes.

Chapter 5: Tales of Dark and Malevolent Shamans

Matinta-Perera: Devious People Turn into Birds

*A*couple had a small store where Brazilian nut gatherers and loggers purchased supplies. One day, a fellow who had just moved into the same town brought an owlet to the store. One of the couple's children fell in love with the bird and wanted it for his own. The man, who made his living by carving animals in wood, didn't want to part with his owlet because it had been the gift of some friends of his, loggers by profession. But the child begged so much that the man gave him the bird under the condition that he could visit it any time.

One of the servants crossed herself when she saw the owlet. "It's a Matinta-perera," the servant said, "a bird that allows a person or shaman to take its body to harass the villagers in the forest."

"*Essas são besteiras dos índios*!" exclaimed the storekeeper's wife, "That's just a silly native tale." She took the owlet and put it in the aviary with her other birds. There the bird was happy, well fed on leftover meat; it also liked bread and milk that its previous owner brought. He worked in his little wood-carving shop until late at night.

Time passed, and as the servant had warned, the villagers began to hear piercing whistles that disturbed everyone's sleep and made the animals restless. Whoever or whatever it was that had transformed into a bird flew in the dark after midnight and disappeared before the villagers could shout at the owlet: "*Cumpadre venha tomar café amanhã bem cedo*. Friend, come by for coffee early tomorrow morning." This invitation was designed to reveal the person inside the bird in the sight of those bothered by its cries. Each time they tried their summons, the Matinta-perera had already vanished.

The servant said to the storekeeper, "Sir, you must know, in the village by the Tocantins River where I used to live, there was an owl who changed into a person, and he was someone who lived right there."

The storekeeper responded, "Go and look. Let me know if you find out what's going on."

That's what she did. When she heard the Matinta-perera close by, she shined a flashlight on the aviary looking for the little owl, but he wasn't there. The next morning while the bird was eating from his cup of milk and bread in the backyard, the maid reported to her employer and repeated that the owl was a Matinta-perera. The man decided to see for himself and spent a night hiding behind a *seringueira*, or rubber tree. Past midnight, when he heard the first whistles coming from the wood carver's shop, the storekeeper shouted, *"Cumpadre venha tomar café amanhã bem cedo.* Friend, come by for coffee early tomorrow morning." He went back to his house and looked in the aviary; the owl wasn't there.

The next day, the wood carver came to the store, shamefacedly answering the invitation to coffee.

The notion of people and shamans who can turn into animals underlies this tale. Other versions of this myth, common in many towns in the Brazilian Amazon, present the Matinta-perera as an old woman who likes to chew tobacco and fly around at night. In such tales, people reveal her identity by yelling to her as she flies through the air, inviting her to come for tobacco the next day.

Pusanga: Love Ointment

$\mathcal{T}$ here was a pretty woman in Iquitos, Peru, whose husband was a rich merchant. One day, she was on her way home on a boat coming from the village of Nauta, and she passed the time talking to a very nice young man. "I am from Lima," he said, "but I'm traveling through the forest villages to trade for animal hides."

The woman didn't realize that the young man was flirting with her.

He was sly, and each time he ran into a woman he liked, he made it a point to be charming to arouse her interest. But he realized that attracting the attention of this woman was not going to be easy, because she was very loyal to her husband. Nevertheless, the persistent young man decided to get off the boat with her in Iquitos. There he found out that the woman spent a great deal of the time with her husband, who had a store selling outboard engines, fishing tackle, and tools for working in the forest.

This challenge didn't stop the young man. He began to show up in the store, pretending to be interested in buying tools for a small farm he was clearing on one of the rivers. He struck up a conversation with the shop owner about the possibility of doing some business, thereby finding an excuse to come in more frequently.

One day, the merchant had to make a trip to the Yavari River, which meant he would be gone for a few weeks. During the husband's absence, the young man took the opportunity to tell the woman that he was crazy about her. "I don't know what I'll do if you don't return my love," he said.

"Don't be a fool," said the woman. "I love my husband."

When her husband returned, the woman wanted to tell him about this episode but decided not to. She was afraid because her husband was easily enraged and would accuse her of being interested in the young man and beat her, as he did each time another man admired her.

Instead, she told the story to one of her servants. The servant was the wife of a fisherman, well-known for being faithful to her husband. "Be very careful," the servant said. "The young man might cast a spell on you."

The young fellow thought of himself as quite the lady's man and was hurt by this woman's refusal. He swore to himself that he would have her no matter what. He went to villages deep in the forest where he knew men and women who were good at magic perfumes and love potions. There he made a deal with a witch doctor, telling him that he was willing to pay anything for the woman to fall for him. The witch doctor assured him that he would be able to help him with an ointment he made for such cases. He told the man to come back in two weeks when the new moon appeared.

When the young man returned, the witch doctor gave him some ointment and said, "The only thing you need to do is to find a way to rub this on the woman. Then you should leave town for a week so she can't see you."

Taking the ointment, the young man asked, "What is it made of?"

"It is made of the blood of a black she-dog; the other ingredients are secrets I can't tell you about, but I assure you, it never fails."

The young man returned to Iquitos and began to visit the store again.

At first, he talked to the husband about business in the forest, and he behaved respectfully to the woman. He repeated these visits, talking business and acting like an honest man for a few weeks, until he got the woman to trust him again.

During this time, the mayor of Iquitos gave a big party to which the woman and her husband were invited. When the young man found this out, he managed to get himself invited, too. At the party everyone had a few drinks, and as things got more lively, the young man went to where the woman and her husband were sitting and asked if he could dance a Peruvian waltz with her. While they were dancing, the young man rubbed some of the love potion on her hand and her bare back.

The next day, as the witch doctor had advised, he left town for one week. In the meantime, the woman began to be annoyed by her husband. She stopped accompanying him to the store and cooking for him and began to frequent the young man's favorite bars. The woman, once known for her virtue, wasn't the same. Now it was she who was chasing the young man.

Her husband grew suspicious and beat her many times to bring her back to her senses, but she no longer wanted her house or her husband; so she left. She went to live with her young man, and they stayed together for some time.

After a while, the young man abandoned her.

The servant who had warned her no longer worked for the merchant because in his rage, he fired all the servants, sold everything, and went away. She used to say, "I told her that young man was going to put a *pusanga*, or magical spell, on her. Just imagine! She didn't believe me. I've been with my husband for over ten years and can't leave him, because he has secured me with a very strong pusanga from a pink dolphin."

As for the woman, she ran around with other men until she lost her beauty.

The use of plants and animal organs to make love potions and ointments is common in the Amazon. These products, known as pusangas, can be purchased along with medicinal plants in most Amazonian markets, including those in major cities such as Iquitos, Manaus, and Belém de Pará. Since the dolphin is considered to have seductive powers, its eyes, fat, and genitalia are sold in markets and used by people to attract lovers. In the Madeira River, it is believed that if you look at a person through a dolphin's eye, he or she will fall in love with you.

CHAPTER 6

Tales of Punishment
for Ill Behavior

Lamparilla: Glowing Ghost

$\mathcal{T}$here once was a schoolteacher from Lima, Peru, who went to work at a little school on the Tapiche River. Since he was an only child, he took good care of his mother, but he loved going to parties and drank a bit too much. The people in the village thought he had a good heart, so they warned him about the *Lamparilla*, the glowing ghost who had killed a drunkard a short time before.

The man did not believe them and made fun of their warnings. "Those stories are for peasants, not for me," he said. One night during Carnaval,[1] he had a few drinks and was walking along a trail by the banks of the Tapiche while thinking of the fun he had had at the party. After half an hour on the trail, he sensed that someone or something was following him. He thought it might be people coming from the party. But soon he realized that what was following him was like a person with a light at the height of his chest. It was like a giant firefly. At this point he was very frightened, for he remembered being told that evil spirits are on the loose during Carnaval.

The man tried to call for help but couldn't, for no words would come.

So he continued walking. The light followed him at the same pace. When he stopped, the light would disappear. But as soon as he resumed walking, the light seemed to come after him. He began to look back, walking faster and faster. The light began closing in on him from all directions, jumping from his left to his right. This continued for some time, until the man decided to stop again, and say a prayer to God to protect him from whatever evil this might be. After he finished his prayer, he began to hear the voices of some people who were coming from the party.

In the presence of the people, the Lamparilla couldn't kill him. It turned its back on him and disappeared over the waters of the Tapiche River. Seeing how shaken the man was, his friends asked him what had happened, and comforted him. When he got home, he told his mother of the strange occurrence, and said he was very lucky.

After that, the man stopped getting drunk and hanging out until dawn. One night, after some time had passed, something called out from his dreams. "What were you doing alone on that trail at that hour of the night?" asked a voice.

"I was coming back from a party," the man answered in his dream.

"Well," replied the voice, "it is very dangerous to be outside at that hour. Had you been a bad person, I would have taken your soul away and today you and I would be roaming that trail together every night."

This story, told by a woman washing clothes and others in and around Iquitos, forms part of the lore that condemns bad behavior and serves to affirm moral codes against excessive use of alcohol. As in many oral narratives about supernatural forest and river creatures, spirits are able to communicate with victims through dreams.

---

[1]**Carnaval:** A celebration with a typical dance performed in the Peruvian Amazon around *humishas*, or trees decorated with small mirrors, pennants, gifts, and sometimes live animals that people take home at the end of the celebration.

Runamula: Women of Ill Repute Turn into Mules

*J*n one of the towns on the Amazon River, people began hearing the sounds of a mule galloping through the streets every Friday after midnight. They could tell by the sound of the hooves and the neighing that the rider was lashing the mule in order to leave town as quickly as possible.

"These neighs are not from a regular mule," said an old man from the town. "They must be from a *Runamula*." According to him, when a woman is not loyal to her husband, her body turns into a mule and is ridden by a demon until dawn. In the morning, the mule turns back into the woman. The lashes from the demon's whip are so harsh that they leave marks on the woman's body, forcing her to stay in bed so people can't see her wounds. To find out who the Runamula is, all you have to do is to look for the scars left on her body. Sometimes this is hard, because these women know how to conceal their wounds.

A boy who had just come to town heard the story of the Runamula and repeated it to his uncle, who had been a healer in a settlement in the forest. The old man told him that another way of recognizing the Runamula was to throw a pot full of *huito*, black dye obtained from a tree, at her as she galloped by; the next day, the woman would have her face stained black from the huito. But he also said that if he were brave, he could catch the Runamula using a seven-colored lasso.

"Caught with this lasso around her neck and tied to a banana tree," he said, "she will lose all her strength. You could grow rich from such a capture because you can ask the demon on her back for a ransom. The demons always carry saddlebags full of gold and silver."

The boy decided to try to catch the Runamula; and he waited for her with a seven-colored lasso at the end of town near some banana trees. When the Runamula got close enough, he threw his lasso. Caught, the Runamula lost all her strength, and it was easy to tie her to a banana tree. Then, as his uncle had instructed him, he said to the demon who was riding her, "Now that I have captured one of your souls, you must pay for her release with gold and silver. Otherwise, I will leave her tied up so that the people will beat her in the morning."

The demon didn't want the Runamula to be caught and forced to repent for her sins, so he gave the boy the saddlebags full of gold and silver. Once the boy got what he had asked for, he ran away, but forgot to untie the Runamula. The next day, the neighbors found a woman tied by her neck to a banana tree. The demon was gone, and the boy and his wise uncle had disappeared, too.

Some say they went to the Ucayali River, where they bought a canoe and became prosperous fishmongers.

In the Peruvian Amazon, people recount the story of a supernatural mule whose galloping keeps them awake at night. The many variations of the tale refer to cases of dissolute women who have intimate relationships with priests, close relatives, or neighbors. Most versions incorporate the use of the huito tree (Genipa americana) *to reveal the woman's identity; this plant also is used as food and to dye clothing.*

Cowboy Quemdera

Told by an Amazonian cowboy from the island of Marajó on the Amazon River in Brazil.

"Quemdera, the spirit of a cowboy who died in a cattle roundup, now wanders through the island of Marajó, either guiding other cowboys on their way home from parties or getting them lost if he chooses."

In Cachoeira do Arari, on Marajó Island, Brazil, among stories like the one about the mother of fire, the man who turned into a horse, and others, people tell the tale of a cowboy favored by Quemdera. This cowboy, who lived on one of the ranches with his mother, was well-liked by the owner, who paid him with sheep, buffalos, horses, ducks, and pigs that he also allowed the cowboy to keep and raise on the owner's land. The cowboy would get up at 4 AM to chop firewood, milk the cows, and herd cattle. Everyone liked him. He was faulted only for his habit of going to parties at other ranches to drink *leite de onça* (buffalo milk loaded with alcohol) in excess and play dominoes.

His mother, who worked in the ranch's kitchen, worried about her son and warned him not to go out so much, for something bad could happen to him in the armed brawls the cowboys had at the parties. Her son usually beat the other cowboys in dominoes and took everything they owned. His mother, to save him from his vices, would go to religious celebrations in Cachoeira do Arari to pray to the patron saint of cowboys, Nossa Senhora da Conceição. But her son did not heed his mother's warnings. He kept coming home drunk from the parties, and claimed that when the nights were dark and the stars tried to get him lost, Quemdera, the cowboy guardian, appeared by his side on his white horse and guided him.

One day, his mother begged her son not to go to one of the parties because a *Macumbeira*, or female shaman, who had a lot of knowledge because of her relationship with the spirits of the dead, had warned her for him to stay home.

The cowboy wanted to go anyway.

That night, the leite de onça that the men and women liked flowed freely. But since he had been warned by his mother, instead of drinking with the other cowboys, that night he danced with all the women without asking permission from the men. Then he finally gave in and played dominoes with the other cowboys. He beat them all, one by one, and took everything they had—even their horses. Everyone was envious and wanted to do him harm, but the cowboy defended himself. He even beat one of the men with a *muxinga*, a whip that herders use on cattle and to punish pigs that damage plants in the orchards.

Later, the cowboy left the party. But he did not arrive at the ranch, nor did he awake to chop firewood at 4 AM as he was supposed to do. When his friends realized he was gone, they searched until they found him asleep under an *açaí* palm grove, clearly headed in a different direction from the ranch where he lived. Since they had always been convinced that he was favored by Quemdera, they didn't consider that the roaming spirit had been the one that misled him. His mother said prayers and gave thanks to Nossa Senhora da Conceição for having saved her son. His other cowboy friends also thanked the virgin saint of the cowboys.

Several days passed, and the Macumbeira, who the spirits had warned about the fate of the cowboy, told his mother, "Look, I also believe in our Nossa Senhora da Conceição, but it was not her who helped your son." She said that after the argument, other cowboys had wanted to kill him. The cowboy he had beaten with the muxinga had gone to wait for him on the pathway to his ranch with the other cowboys who had sharpened their *facas*, or knives, to cut him to pieces. "Quemdera does not want him to be killed. He got him lost so he would not be hurt," the Macumbeira said.

"That's just like Quemdera," say the cowboys who still tell stories at night at the O Paraiso ranch on the road to Cachoeira do Arari. "Quemdera wanders on horseback at night through the island's pastures during the dry season, guiding the cowboys he likes and confusing those he doesn't so they become lost."

Multiple variations of this tale are told by Amazonian cowboys and people in haciendas close to Cachoeira do Arari who swore to have seen this cowboy's ghost riding on a white horse through the savannas on the island of Marajó during the dry season. This story, different from those originating from forest lore in which spirits are invoked to explain mysteries, utilizes the presence of a Macumbeira, or female shaman, subscribing to the African religious traditions of Marajó, Belém de Pará, and nearby regions in the Brazilian Amazon.

Caballococha: A Town Plagued by Ill Behavior

*C*aballococha literally means "lake of horses" in Spanish. Many years ago, the town of Caballococha wasn't called by that name. It was a place where many people had become rich selling fine wood, animal skins, and enslaving the native people. There were parties, people drunk in the streets, and men stealing other men's wives.

One day, a little old man appeared in town and said, "If you don't change this way of life, something terrible is going to happen."

But nobody, except for the servants and a few fishermen, paid attention to him. The others who heard this just laughed at him. Soon after, at an event hosted by a rich lumber merchant, the partygoers were surprised by the appearance of two white horses neighing loudly on the patio of the house. Some were afraid because they knew there were no horses in this part of the Amazon, but they were too drunk to think of the warnings they had been given.

However, the servants remembered the words of the old man; and they ran out of the house yelling to everyone about the two horses. When they saw the lake full of waves and roaring like a fierce beast, and the waters of the lake begin to foam, they ran to save their families.

Before dawn, while many were still partying, the lake swallowed the prosperous settlement—its bars and brothels, along with most of the beautiful houses and chest after chest of gold and silver. Only the servants who had seen the two white horses and a few fishermen were able to escape.

Several weeks later, the servants and their families, who had taken refuge in the fishermen's huts, started to build a new town. The lake that had acted like a beast became quiet again, and *gramalote*, a type of grass, grew around it. Since then, many have searched in vain for the gold and silver that the lake devoured that night.

Tourists and the inhabitants of Caballococha say that just before dusk they can see the two white horses grazing on the shore of the lake from their windows. "But if you try to get closer to them," they say, "the horses will disappear into the lake."

This story is told by people of all ages in Caballococha, a town situated in the Peruvian Amazon near the Colombian border. The tale alludes to the riches obtained by the extraction of natural resources and inhumane treatment of indigenous people and incorporates the belief of Amazonians that there are supernatural animals and spirits inhabiting bodies of water. The immorality and arrogance of the inhabitants provokes punishment from spirits of nature.

CHAPTER 7

Tales of Special Places, Plants, and Birds

The Enchanted City

A boy from Iquitos, Peru, joined a group of loggers in the forest. He traveled with them up the Nanay River where they worked cutting down marketable *caoba* and *cedro* trees. He worked hard to save, and to give money to his parents. In the afternoon, while his friends played cards, he would sit on the riverbanks lost in his thoughts.

One day, he met a beautiful girl walking on the riverbank, and they fell in love. He told her about the Alhambra Theater in Iquitos and the ice cream vendors in the plaza.

"You'd be amazed at the city I'm from," the girl replied. "I would love to take you to meet my family." She described the city for him, saying that it was a place where people didn't kill themselves with work. The houses were lovely and the pantries full of food, and meals were served on plates of gold decorated with precious stones. "If you want, we can go there tomorrow," she said.

The boy agreed, and the next day the girl led him by the hand to a big stone door guarded by a *chacruna*, a shrub known for its magical powers. The girl said some magic words to the plant, and the door opened. They went through a tunnel leading to a river, down which they traveled to a door guarded by two *renaco* trees with boas wrapped around their branches. The girl whistled to the boas, and they uncoiled to let the couple pass. They then climbed stone steps to a valley where lay a city of stone. It looked like it was built by the Incas.

The splendor of the place impressed the boy deeply. He enjoyed strolling down the paved avenues lined with fountains where people bathed in order to cure illness and extend their lives. He was happy, and he didn't realize how long a time he had been away from his family and his friends the loggers.

He thought so much about the life he had left behind that he told the girl, "You know how much I love you, but I must return to the logging camp and send news to my parents in Iquitos."

She agreed and accompanied him, telling him she would wait for him not very far away.

The boy arrived at the camp, which had by that time been moved farther up the river. When his friends saw him, they were astonished, for they thought he had drowned.

They told him that his relatives had combed the forest searching for him. Then he told his friends so much about the girl and the city that they thought he was crazy.

"How could you abandon your life here and leave us to go with that woman? She might be a ghost or a devil."

He assured them that she was a woman from this world; he said he was happy and had returned only to ask them a favor. He wanted them to take his parents a letter and a leather bag. They agreed, and he returned to the city.

After he left, one of his friends, overcome by curiosity, opened the bag. It was full of nuggets of gold and precious stones. They left the camp and looked for the boy down many trails, but never found him.

Stories of rich cities in the forest, reminiscent of the legends of El Dorado and the Gran Paititi, are based on the belief that the Amazon is a land of extraordinary wealth. The conquistadors and new inhabitants of the Amazon, who heard the native people tell of the riches and then took them, recreated illusions and nostalgia for old wealth through new tales. Versions of this story were heard from women workers and passengers on a boat that traveled between Caballococha and Iquitos.

Renacal: A Grove of Magical Trees

One day, a few men wanted to go fishing in one of the lakes near the Samiria River in the Peruvian Amazon. They were planning to catch a lot of fish and salt them for Lent. The father-in-law of one of the men who knew the lakes and rivers told them, "Be careful. Once, a giant anaconda surprised a friend of mine and turned over his canoe. He was almost eaten for trying to fish there. In that lake, the anaconda owns the fish and doesn't like people. I wouldn't go there."

The men were very cocky, and didn't pay him much attention.

They got their tackle ready and arrived at the lake in the afternoon. They camped across from an island of renaco trees full of vines that was a good fishing spot. That night while they were sleeping, there was a great storm, but they weren't worried because they took shelter between the roots of a big tree.

Early the next morning, the island was nowhere in sight.

They searched for it everywhere, and by sunset, they realized that they had gone all around the lake. They set up camp again where they had been the night before. The next day, a light breeze and the chirping of many birds woke them.

The island had reappeared and was slowly coming toward them, until it stopped not far from shore.

One of the men said, "I dreamed of a very tall woman who came out of the renaco grove with little anacondas for fingers that caught fish for her. She said she was the owner of this lake and that all of it—the fish, the renacos, the animals—came from her body. She also said that we should fish somewhere else."

But the others were foolhardy and said that they were not going to be swayed by dreams or stories. "We're not leaving this place until we catch and salt all the fish we can get," said one of them. They spent the entire morning fishing, trying not to get too close to the island or to bother the boas that were curled up in the renacos sleeping. Toward noon, when they had caught a lot of fish, a very strong wind blowing across the lake threatened to drown them on their fishing raft.

They tried to cope with the storm but were unable.

In the midst of the lightning and the rain, the island of the renacos began to move, first slowly, then more quickly. The island, like a ship of renacos, in whose roots lived dolphins, turtles, manatees, and all kinds of fish, disappeared in the darkness lit by flashes of lightning, accompanied by thunder and rain.

The men were barely able to pole to shore.

They left all of their things at the camp and ran back to town, where they told the story of what had happened to them.

This tale told by fishermen from the Samiria River portrays the common fear of fishing in areas with large groves of renaco trees. The ghostly landscape presented by a renaco grove leads people to believe in the existence of spirits who protect the places where animals rest or lay eggs. In many instances, especially in the past among indigenous people, fear of these spirits has eased the human pressure on some areas of the forests and river systems as it helps to diminish hunting and fishing activities.

Boa Plants: Plants Turn into Animals

*O*n the banks of the Huallaga River, in the Peruvian Amazon, there lived a newly married couple who had two small planters full of what everyone called boa plants that had been a present from an uncle who lived in the forest. These plants not only brought good luck to the house, but also scared away rats and bats. With thin, tiny leaves, the female plant climbed from her pot to a beam near the door that led to the street. The male plant, which was bigger and had robust leaves, wrapped around a kitchen column. As time passed, the couple began to be awakened at night by the smooth sound of leaves moving. They saw the plants taking the form of two boa constrictor snakes and slowly unwinding themselves from the columns and heading toward the yard. There, they got into the pond, which contained some *charapa* and *cupiso* turtles and a renaco tree that the first inhabitants of the house had left. The boa plants would shine in the moonlight and whistle beside the turtles. Since the couple did not have children, they enjoyed waking up at night to watch the plants turn into boas. In the morning, the woman never missed watering the plants so that their leaves stayed healthy and shiny.

Time passed, and the couple had to move to Iquitos, because of the man's job. The woman wanted to take the boa plants along, but she worried that the move might kill them. She decided it would be better to discuss the matter with the lady who would be moving into the house and to ask her to give them water and put compost in their pots from time to time.

She offered to pay her and the other woman agreed. The couple moved and adjusted to their new life, but they missed their old house with the boa plants and the pool with its turtles in the yard. Whenever the woman returned to the Huallaga to visit her family, she asked the new tenant how the plants were doing. The woman living in the house told her that she had to convince her husband to let her keep the plants.

"My husband was very upset at first," said the woman, "because he thought they were the devil's plants, but I convinced him that plants that had the ability to turn into boas would help run off the rats and would bring good luck." She also said that when her little son would not stop crying at night when there was a full moon, she would take

---

him out to the yard so that he could see the boa plants playing in the water with the turtles. The woman from Iquitos was delighted that the boa plants were still useful, and on her return, she brought the good news to her husband.

Later, when the woman returned again to Huallaga, she asked about the boa plants; the new occupant told her that everything was going fine. The couple from Iquitos was very grateful. But one day, the woman returned to her old house and could not find the boa plants; the pool was gone and where the renaco tree had been, the house had more rooms. The woman wanted to think that the boa plants had gone to live in one of the lakes near the town.

When she asked the woman of the house about the boa plants, she was told that one night her husband (who now lived with another woman) had come home drunk and destroyed them. She said, "One night he found them stowed away together in a big cistern and went crazy, screaming 'things of the devil, things of the devil.' Then he hit them so many times with a machete that the kitchen walls were covered with blood. The next day," she continued, "there was not even a drop of blood; only the tiny pieces of their dried earthen leaves."

This story is founded on the notion that animals and plants have a spirituality that allows them to change their external shape, or "clothing." According to indigenous mythologies, animals and other beings can alter their external appearance simply by exchanging their "clothes" for those of whatever they wish to become. The story also underlines indigenous and mestizo belief that boas bring good luck to people. In fact, many believe that boas have a stone in their heads that brings good luck, especially in business.

Ayaymama: A Bird Who Cries Like a Human

*O*ne day, a man who lived with his wife and two children in the forest went hunting, but never returned. To keep her children from being sad, the woman told them that their father would be home soon. Since she wanted to look for him, she told them she was going into the forest to collect wood and fruit.

Thinking their father had abandoned them and that their mother was planning to do the same, the brother and sister started to cry. Their mother assured them that she would not desert them for anything in the world, and then went looking for her husband, beating tree trunks and calling for him. The woman faithfully continued her search for many days without losing hope. Unfortunately, she was killed by a *jergón* snake.

When the children realized their mother was not coming back, they decided to go into the forest to search for her. Tearfully, they called out, *"Ayaymama, Ayaymama, huischurchuarca?"* ("Dear mother, dear mother, why have you abandoned us?") The forest animals took pity on the children. The *maquisapa* monkeys threw fruit and delicious seeds and the *paucar* birds imitated other birds to cheer them up. Thanks to these and other animals that protected them, the children survived. They could walk through the forest without being bitten by snakes or attacked by ferocious forest cats.

The children wandered among the trees and spent more and more days and nights in the branches. Living among the leaves and the vines, they saw their hair had begun to turn into feathers; they were like most of their new friends who had feathers. Also, their arms turned into wings, and feathers grew all over their bodies. Eventually, they began to fly and to live permanently in the treetops. That's where they still live.

The people in Santa Elena say that the solitude of the forest makes the children sad, and at night they can be heard crying from the trees: *"Ayaymama, Ayaymama, huischurchuarca?"*

This story, which has many varieties in the Peruvian Amazon, is related to the ayaymama *(Nyctibius griseus), whose nocturnal singing sounds like a child crying for his mother deep in the forest. This tale may have been influenced by the Brothers Grimm's* Hansel and Gretel.

Lupuna: A Tree Becomes Vengeful

A few loggers working in the forest near Atacuari, in the Colombian Amazon, hadn't been able to transport their wood from cedro, canela moena, and comino trees because the creeks leading to the river were almost dry. To make it rain that night, one of them beat the trunk of a big-bellied lupuna tree. But the rain never came. Instead, the next day the logger who had beaten the lupuna began to have stomach pains.

The pains were so bad, he could not walk, and his stomach began to swell.

His friends were worried, so they called a shaman. The shaman visited the lupuna the logger had beaten and realized that the poor man had beaten the wrong tree—a red one, also called lupuna colorada, whose mother lives in its belly. The shaman told the man that he had gone about it the wrong way.

"Not only did you fail to greet the Lupuna before beating her, but you also used her trunk as a bathroom. You should never have treated the tree in such a way, exposing her to your filthiness," the shaman said.

Upon hearing this, the logger was very afraid, for his stomach had become so big that he couldn't get out of bed. He thought sadly of his wife and children. The shaman told him not to worry, and he promised that he would beg the lupuna's mother to withdraw her evil spell. He assured him that if it were necessary, he would fight her. "If I win the fight," said the shaman, "you will get well. If I can't break the spell, your stomach will grow bigger and bigger until it explodes."

The shaman armed himself with a few bottles of *aguardiente* (sugarcane liquor) and some tobacco, and went to talk to the lupuna's mother. She was an old woman; her hair was made out of little leaves and she had a face carved in wood. The mother of the tree looked at him with eyes of fire and told him that the logger had urinated on the trunk of her house. "Because of his actions, the logger will die with his stomach swollen, " she snarled.

To gain strength and bravery, the shaman began to smoke and drink. Around midnight, he called the jaguar and the anaconda to help him in his battle and returned to the camp to wait. The jaguar ripped at the tree trunk with his powerful claws, and the anaconda wrapped herself around the tree's belly and squeezed.

Near dawn, the men of the camp heard an enormous explosion. "That was the Lupuna's mother. My friends the anaconda and the jaguar forced her to leave the trunk," said the shaman. That afternoon, the logger's stomach began to return to normal and he was able to get up. His friends who hadn't been able to transport the wood went to beat a white lupuna tree, the kind whose mother doesn't get angry, to bring rain.

The logger was very grateful to the shaman, and he decided to visit the lupuna whose mother had punished him. Once there, he placed beside her trunk a little box in which he had put some candy and soft drinks.

Many tales exist in which lupuna trees are used by evil shamans to do harm to people. It is said that shamans make a hole in the tree's "belly" and deposit bits of leftovers from the victim's plate and wait for him to die as his stomach swells up and explodes. In such cases, to save the victim, another, more powerful shaman should go to the tree and make a ritualistic incision into its belly.

Chicua: Messenger Bird

On the Amazon River near Puerto Nariño, a man and his wife lived on a small plot of land. The man grew *batata*, or sweet potatoes and plantains. He also grew manioc, from which he and his wife made farinha[1] to sell to merchants from the boats. One day when the man was going to weed his crops, he heard the persistent song of the chicua bird. "Chic-chic-chicua," sang the little bird with tiny red eyes, perched close by on the branches of the bushes beside the trail.

People say the chicua sings "chic-chic-chicua" to warn of some misfortune. But the man paid no attention, and the repetitious song of the bird started to annoy him. "Chic-chic-chicua," sang the bird, small and dark, jumping in front of him in the bushes. Later, in his plot garden, as the little bird continued bothering him with his song, the man began to yell at him to leave him alone. After a string of scoldings and insults, the little bird stopped singing and the man worked in peace. At sunset, nevertheless, when the man started on his way home, on the pathway the bird repeated his annoying "chic-chic-chicua." Again, the man yelled at the little bird until he left him alone.

In his house, the man found his wife and everything to be just like always.

The next day, again on his way to work, the man heard the little bird accompanying him with his "chic-chic-chicua." The man scolded him just like the day before. "Stop bugging me—go bother someone else! Can't you see I have a lot to do!" He screamed furiously, throwing chunks of mud and sticks at the bird. But it was no use. The little bird followed him everywhere, dodging the sticks and mud thrown at him, jumping from one branch to another, getting closer and closer to the man and looking at him with his restless little eyes, singing "chic-chic-chicua."

The man was filled with rage and screamed, "What do you want? If you're a person, just come out and tell me what's going on, but don't bother me all day long—you are keeping me from my work." When the man spoke these words, the bird turned into a man and told him, "Look, if you want, I am going to make you see, as in a mirror, what is happening in your home." The man told him that an acquaintance was coming to his house each day to see his wife while he was at work. Then the man turned back into a chicua. The offended husband stopped what he was doing and ran for home.

While he was running, all along the path he heard "chic-chic-chicua," and it grew louder and louder.

When he arrived at his home, just as the little bird had said, he found his wife betraying him with one of the farinha dealers who did business with the people on the riverbanks. Humiliated by his wife and the other man, he could not contain himself. He killed them with an ax right on the spot. The news spread up and down the river, and the authorities came and took him to be judged in Leticia. The case did not take very long, since the man had acted out of passion arising from his wife's betrayal.

He was pardoned and allowed to return to his house.

A little while later, on the path to his little farm, the man heard once again the song of the chicua: "chic-chic-chic." This time the man did not say anything. Then the little bird shook his tail and jumped in front of him, turning himself into the same man who had appeared the day of his betrayal, and said, "Look, man, please don't insult me, don't ever chide me again. If it is going to rain and ruin your crops, I will warn you with my singing. If the river is going to betray you, I will tell you ahead of time. If a terrible thing is going to happen to you, I get sad, too. And that's why I ask you to never insult me again, please never chide me again."

The chicua (Piaya cayana) is a bird thought to deliver omens by people from the upper Ucayali and Marañón rivers and for those who live as far away as Marajó Island at the mouth of the Amazon in the Atlantic Ocean. Some shamans believe that the chicua's song pattern of "chic-chic-chic" signals good fortune, while its song pattern "chic-chic-chicua" is a bad omen. Many believe that if children eat chicua brains, they will become very intelligent.

---

[1]**Farinha:** A type of flour made from the tuber of the manioc plant. An important food staple for Amazonians.

Pumayuyu: A Plant with Magical Powers

*T*he people of Puerto Napo, in the Ecuadorian Amazon, tell the story of a little old lady who was more than 120 years old and who was much loved by her family. Her granddaughters took care of her and she was never without her half cup of tea made out of pumayuyu, a plant with curly leaves that grew in the backyard. The old lady was blind, but she was so healthy that sometimes she went a whole week without eating, and everyone was glad to see her with so much energy.

One day, one of her granddaughters noticed a wound on her leg. The young woman was alarmed and when she asked her grandmother what had happened, the little old lady said that she had cut herself on one of the table's benches in the night. The granddaughter believed her, and since her grandmother was so old, she told her to call for help the next time she needed to get up at night. Weeks went by, and the old lady with her fasting not only was cured, but became even healthier.

The granddaughter began thinking that something strange was going on. She said to herself, "I am going to see who is bringing her food at night."

She stayed hidden in the backyard while looking through the kitchen window. From there, she watched the old lady get up and walk easily toward the kitchen as if she were a girl. In the darkness, her grandmother's eyes shone like a cat's as she went through the kitchen and out the back door into the yard.

Curious, the granddaughter followed her. In the full moon, her grandmother's fingernails transformed into claws and she changed into a jaguar. The jaguar went down the path close to the chicken coops, avoiding one of the grandsons who was standing guard with a rifle in case any jaguars or foxes came to eat the chickens.

The next day, the girl told her brothers and her mother what she had seen, and the family consulted a wise Yachak[2] to find out what was wrong with their grandmother.

With the aid of wanduc, as people in the Ecuadorian Amazon call this visionary plant, and with other plants, he told them not to worry about her or her health, that if she died it would be of old age. "Because her parents were so wise as to give her good pumayuyu juice since she was a child, she will never be sick. The juice turns her into a jaguar at night," said the wise man.

Since they knew that, thanks to the pumayuyu, their grandmother was healthy and would turn into a jaguar at night, they didn't worry about her anymore, and the men stopped guarding the chicken coops so that they wouldn't accidentally hurt her.

Eventually, death came from heaven and the old lady died peacefully. Her family gave her a Christian burial and later, relatives brought flowers to her grave every week. This went on until one day one of the granddaughters went to visit and found that something had dug a hole in her grave.

"It was as if an animal had dug in to eat her remains, or as if someone had tried to rob her bones to do witchcraft," said the priest and some others. But her relatives were not worried anymore, because the Yachak had told them: "The pumayuyu turns her into a jaguar and after death she still roams this world."

Then the relatives had a very happy party and celebrated that their grandmother was now walking freely and eating the best meat in the forest.

Variations of this story praising the powers of pumayuyu (Teliostachya lanceolata) and other medicinal plants are told by indigenous and mestizo inhabitants in the Tena area of the Ecuadorian Amazon. This story also illustrates the importance of hunting game, a source of protein currently under pressure due to continued deforestation and development by oil industries in the region.

---

[2]**Yachak**: A word used for shaman in the Napo area of the Amazonian Ecuador.

GLOSSARY OF VERNACULAR AND SCIENTIFIC NAMES

Açaí (*Euterpe oleracea* Mart.): Assai palm. Palm tree member of the euterpe family, from which hearts of palm and juice are obtained. Known as *huasai* palm in Peru.

Aguaje (*Mauritia flexuosa* L.f.): Palm tree commonly found in swampy wetlands that produces bunches of small, reddish, edible fruits.

Anaconda (*Eunectes murinus*): A serpent of extraordinary muscular strength that lives in the water and swampy areas of South America and reaches a length of up to twelve meters. It is carnivorous, feeding on fish and mammals such as deer, capibara, and tapirs when they approach rivers to drink water. It is an animal of semiaquatic habits and is different from the boa constrictor, which lives and hunts mainly in trees and dry areas.

Anta (*Tapirus terrestris*): The biggest mammal of the Amazonian forest and one of the four species of the tapir family. It weighs up to 500 pounds and its meat is consumed by Amazonians. Other vernacular names for this mammal are *sacha-vaca* and *danta*.

Ayahuasca (*Banisteriopsis caapi*): Also called the vine of the soul, it is used to make a hallucinogenic beverage that is consumed by indigenous people and mestizos in Amazonia. Shamans drink it during special ceremonies in order to communicate with spirits of the forest.

Ayaymama (*Nyctibius griseus*): Great Potoo. Pale grey to brown bird that inhabits tropical America and makes deep gutteral sounds.

Balatá (*Manilkara bidentata*): A hardwood tree that produces heavy red timber and balata gum used for fabrication of golf balls.

Boruga (*Agouti paca*): Paca. A medium-sized rodent that lives in tropical and subtropical areas of the Americas. Is one of the most-prized game animals among Amazonians. Also known as *majaz, majás,* and *lapa*.

Bujeo (*Inia geoffrensis*): Along with anacondas, one of the most important animals in Amazonian lore. Bujeo is one of several names given to pink dolphins, also known as *botos, bufeos,* and *toninas*. These mammals are born grey and become pink as they grow. Males reach up to three meters (about nine feet) and weigh up to 180 kilograms (about 400 pounds), while females reach two meters (about six feet) and usually weigh 100 kilograms (about 220 pounds). They have a sonar organ in their heads that allows them to hunt in waters with low visibility.

Caimito (*Pouteria caimito*): An oval-shaped fruit with white flesh that grows on a tree of the same name. Closely related to the *zapote* fruit family.

Canela moena (*Aniba canelilla*): Brazilian rosewood. A type of wood used for musical instruments, fine furniture, and decorative pieces. It tends to have an oily texture and a rose-like fragrance.

Caoba (*Swietenia macrophylla*): Mahogany. A tree highly sought after in the Amazon for its valuable wood, almost extinct today.

Capirona (*Calycophyllum spruceanum*): Firewood tree. Its durable, rot-resitant wood is commonly used throughout Amazonia for construction and to make fires.

Castaña (*Bertholletia excelsa*): See *castanheira*.

Castanheira (*Bertholletia excelsa* Humb. & Bonpl.): Brazilian nut tree known for the edible seeds it produces. One of the largest trees in the rain forest, it grows wild throughout the Amazonin basin. Also known as *castaña* or *árbol de castaña*.

Cedro (*Cedrela odorata*): A highly sought after timber tree that grows up to forty meters (130 feet) high in the Amazon rainforest.

Chacruna (*Psychotria viridis*): A chacruna shrub from the coffee family used by *vegetalistas* or healers in the Amazon region.

Charapa (*Podocnemis expansa*): The largest freshwater turtle, the charapa can weight up to forty-five kilograms (about 100 pounds). It lays between eighty and 130 eggs per nest on high sandy beaches. It is also known as the *tartaruga da Amazonia* and *zamurita*.

Chicua: (*Piaya cayana*): This bird is an omen able to warn of rain, a coming disgrace, or a novelty. In some places of Amazonia, it is believed to give advice to shamans.

Comino (*Aniba perutilis* Hemsl.): Tree of fine wood. Virtually extinct due to exceessive cutting.

Copaíba (*Copaifera paupera* Herz.): Midsize tree. From its bark, people obtain a medicinal oil that is used to treat ulcers, wounds, rashes, and dermatitis.

Copoasú (*Theobroma grandiflorum*): A fruit about the size of a melon with large seeds and a creamy pulp that is used by Amazonians to make juice and desserts.

Cupiso (*Podocnemis sextuberculata*): Six-tubercled Amazon river turtle that lays its eggs on river beaches near the water.

Curare (*Chondrodendron tomentosum*): A plant used by indigenous peoples of the Amazon to make poison for their arrows. Its alkaloid tubocurarine is used in modern medicine as a muscle relaxant in surgeries.

Dorado (*Brachyplatystoma rousseauxii*): Gilded catfish, also called *plateado* and *bagre dorado*.

Gamitana (*Colossoma macropomum* Cuvier): A freshwater fish found in the Amazon River, it can reach up to one meter long (three feet) and weigh up to thirty kilograms (about sixty-six pounds). Also known as the *tambaqui*.

Gramalote (*Hymenachne donacifolia*): A type of grass that grows in flooded areas, lakeshores, and riverbanks and serves as food to mammals and fish.

Guaba (*Inga edulis*): Fruits from the guaba tree that contain a sweet, white, cottony pulp enjoyed by people, birds, and monkeys.

Guacharaca (*Ortalis* spp.): A medium-sized bird of light brown color. Well-known by its loud and rough singing in the mornings.

Guama (*Inga edulis*): See *guaba*.

Guazo (*Mazama americana*): Brocket deer.

Huayracaspi (*Cedrelinga catenaeformis*): Also known as the *tornillo*, shamans believe this tree has magical powers. It can be added to ayahuasca hallucenogenic drinks to increase its power.

Huito (*Genipa americana* L.): Small tree growing up to fifteen meters tall (about fifty feet). The juice from its fruit reacts with the skin to produce a black coloring. It is used to make a medicinal tea to treat bronchitis. Also known as *jagua*.

Jergón (*Bothrops atrox*): Highly venemous South American pit viper and one of the most common in the Amazon.

Jochi pintado (*Agouti paca*): The name used in the Bolivian Amazon for the paca rodent. See *boruga*.

Lupuna colorada (*Cavanillesia hylogeiton*): Red lupuna. A tree found in the Amazon basin with a trunk up to ten meters wide (about thirty-two feet). Lupuna trees are divided into white lupunas and red lupunas. The mother of the white lupuna is said to be generous and provide people with knowledge, while the mother of the red lupuna is dangerous.

Maquisapa (*Ateles belzebuth*): Long-haired spider monkey. It has large limbs and a long tail that allows it to swing in tree branches.

Mutum (*Crax alector*): An edible bird of black feathers also known as *paujil*.

Nacanaca (*Micrurus lemniscatus*): Coral snake.

Onoto (*Bixa orellana* L.): Annatto. Also called *achiote*. Dye obtained from the seeds of a small shrub of the same name. It is used by indigenous people as a magical paint for their bodies in order to prevent atacks from spirits. It is also used by other Amazonians as seasoning and as food coloring.

Pacu (*Piaractus brachypomus*): Red-bellied pacu, a tropical fish of the Amazon River.

Palmito (*Euterpe Spp*): Palmetto. Palm tree from which hearts of palm are harvested and used in salads by Amazonians.

Panguana (*Crypturellus undulatus*): Gray tinamou. Ground bird, sought after by Amazonians because of the delicacy of its meat.

Paucar (*Cacicus* cela): A bird with black and yellow feathers well-known for its ability to imitate the sounds of other birds, some animals, and even humans.

Pintadillo (*Pseudoplatystoma fasciatum*): Tiger shovelnose catfish.

Pirarucú (*Arapaima gigas* Cuvier): Large freshwater fish found in the Amazon basin reaching sizes of three meters and 200 kilograms (about sixteen feet and 440 pounds). Also known as *arapaima* or *paiche*.

Platanillo (*Helioconia bihai*): Lobster claw. Forest dwellers use the leaves from this plant for wrapping food.

Pumayuyu (*Teliostachya lanceolata*): Also known as *toé negro, toé brasilero*, or *maricahua*. Plant with hallucenogenic effects when mixed with ayahuasca.

Renaco (*Ficus americana* Aubl.): Strangler fig. A tree which starts as a vine and grows more vines, embracing its host tree until it ends up strangling it.

Sajino (*Tayassu tajacu*): White-collared peccary found in South America.

Samaúma (*Ceiba pentandra*): Kapok tree, also known as the silk tree and wool tree. Large tree with a buttressed trunk growing in the Amazonian rain forests. It is commonly referred to as *ceiba* and *lupuna blanca*.

Seringa (*Hevea brasiliensis*): Rubber tree.

Seringueira (*Hevea brasiliensis*): Rubber tree.

Shiringa (*Hevea brasiliensis*): Rubber tree.

Toé (*Brugmansia suaveolens*): Hallucinogenic and medicinal plant with trumpet-shaped flowers. Shamans use it alone or as an enhancement to the visionary drink ayahuasca. Known as *yacutoé, borrachero, floripondio, datura*, or *angel's trumpet*.

Tonina (*Inia geoffrensis*): See *bujeo*.

Tucunaré (*Cichla monoculus*): Peacock bass. Large fish found in shallow black waters of the Amazon basin. Its average length is 60 centimeters (23.62 inches) and it weighs about 3 kilograms (6.6 pounds).

Uvilla (*Pourouma cecropiaefolia*): Grape-like fruit from an Amazon tree which has rough skin with white juicy pulp.

Vitória Régia (*Victoria amazonica*): Giant water lily, also known as the Victoria water lily, with leaves that float on top of still waters.

Wanduc: See *toé*.

Yacutoé: See *toé*.

Yarumo (*Cecropia maxima*): A small- to medium-sized tree that grows along the river in Amazonia and is used by natives as fuelwood and for building rafts. Some indigenous cultures of the Amazon burn its leaves for ashes to add to pulverized coca leaves for use in rituals and storytelling sessions. Also known as *cetico*.

Yuca (*Manihot esculenta*): Manioc.

Zapote (*Matisia cordata*): A rounded or elliptical fruit from a tree that grows wild in the rain forest. Other vernacular names are *zapote chupachupa, sapote de monte*, and *sapotillo*.

BIBLIOGRAPHY

Antony, Leandro. *Folclore amazonense*. Manaus, Brazil: Fundação Cultural do Amazonas, 1976.

Bates, Henry Walter. *The Naturalist on the River Amazons*. Santa Barbara, CA: The Narrative Press, 2002.

Brown, Michael F. *Tsewa's Gift: Magic and Meaning in an Amazonian Society*. Washington, D.C.: Smithsonian Institution Press, 1985.

Burga Freitas, Arturo. *Ayahuasca: mitos y leyendas del Amazonas*. Buenos Aires: Editorial Tor, 1939.

Burroughs, William, and Allen Ginsberg. *The Yajé Letters*. San Francisco: City Lights Books, 1963.

Calvo, César. *Las tres mitades de Ino Moxo y otros brujos de la Amazonía*. Iquitos, Perú: Proceso Editores, 1981.

Carvajal, Gaspar de. *Descubrimiento del Río de las Amazonas*. Valencia, Spain: Estudios y Medios, 1992.

Cascudo, Luis da Câmara. *Dicionário do folclore brasileiro*. Rio de Janeiro: Ministério da Educação e Cultura, Instituto Nacional do Livro, 1954.

Cousteau, Jacques Ives. *Jacques Cousteau's Amazon Journey*. New York: N. H. Abrahams, 1984.

Dantas, Amazonina. *Lendas, crendices, estórias do Amazonas*. Rio de Janeiro: Editora Artenova, 1974.

Davis, Wade. *One River: Explorations and Discoveries in the Amazon Rain Forest*. New York: Simon & Schuster, 1996.

Descola, Philippe. *The Spears of Twilight: Life and Death in the Amazon Jungle*. Trans. Janet Lloyd. New York: New Press/HarperCollins Publishers, 1998.

Domínguez, Camilo A. *Amazonía colombiana: visión general*. Bogotá: Fondo de Promoción de la Cultura del Banco Popular, 1985.

Dorson, Mercedes, and Jeanne Wilmot, eds. *Tales from the Rain Forest: Myths and Legends from the Amazonian Indians of Brazil*. New York: The Ecco Press, 1997.

Eliade, Mircea. *Shamanism: Archaic Techniques of Ecstasy*. Princeton, NJ: Princeton University Press, 1964.

Figueroa, Francisco de, Cristobal de Acuña y otros. *Informes de los Jesuitas en el Amazonas*. Iquitos, Perú: IIAP-CETA. Monumenta Amazónica, 1986.

FORMABIAP-AIDESEP. *El ojo verde. Cosmovisiones amazónicas*. Lima: Telefónica del Perú, 2004.

Galeano, Juan Carlos. *Cuentos amazónicos*. Iquitos, Perú: Tierra Nueva Editores, 2007.

Gondim, Neide. *A invenção da Amazônia*. São Paulo: Marco Zero, 1994.

Guevara Yepes, David. *Napo con su propia voz*. Tena, Ecuador: H. Consejo Provincial de Napo, 1995.

Henriquez, Manuel. *Amazonas: Apuntes y crónicas*. Caracas: Ediciones de la Presidencia de la República, Caracas, 1994.

Izquierdo Ríos, Francisco. *Pueblo y bosque: Folklore amazónico*. Lima: P. L. Villanueva, 1975.

La Condamine, Charles-Marie de. *Viaje a la América Meridional por el río de las Amazonas*. Quito: Abya-Yala, 1993.

Lamb, Bruce F. *Wizard of the Upper Amazon: The Story of Manuel Córdoba Ríos*. Boston: Houghton Mifflin Company, 1971.

Lathrap, Donald. *The Upper Amazon*. New York: Praeguer, 1970.

Lévi-Strauss, Claude. *Tristes Trópicos*. Trans. Noelia Bastard. Barcelona: Ediciones Paidós Ibérica, S. A., 1997.

Luna, Luis Eduardo. *Vegetalismo: Shamanism Among the Mestizo Population of the Peruvian Amazon*. Stockholm: Almqvist & Wiksell International, 1986.

Luna, Luis Eduardo, and Pablo Amaringo. *Ayahuasca Visions: The Religious Iconography of a Peruvian Shaman*. Berkeley, CA: North Atlantic Books, 1993.

Luna, Luis Eduardo, and Steven F. White, eds. *Ayahuasca Reader: Encounter with the Amazon's Sacred Vine*. Santa Fe, NM: Synergetic Press, 2000.

Magaña, Edmundo. *Literaturas de los pueblos del Amazonas: una introducción wayana*. Madrid: Editorial MAPFRE, 1992.

Maybury Lewis, David. *Millennium: Tribal Wisdom and the Modern World*. New York: Viking Press, 1992.

Miranda Santos, Theobaldo. *Lendas e mitos do Brasil*. São Paulo: Companhia Editora Nacional, 1974.

Niño, Hugo. *Primitivos relatos contados otra vez*. Habana: Ediciones Casa de las Américas, 1978.

Regan, Jaime. *Hacia la tierra sin mal: Estudio sobre la religiosidad del pueblo en la amazonía*. Iquitos, Perú: CETA, 1983.

Reichel-Dolmatoff, Gerardo. *Amazonian Cosmos: The Sexual and Religious Symbolism of the Tukano Indians*. Chicago: University of Chicago Press, 1971.

Rodríguez de Montes, María Luisa. *Muestra de literatura oral en Leticia, Amazonas*. Bogotá: Instituto Caro y Cuervo, 1981.

Roe, Peter G. *The Cosmic Zygote: Cosmology in the Amazon Basin*. Piscataway; NJ: Rutgers University Press, 1982.

Santos-Granero, Fernando. *The Power of Love: The Moral Use of Knowledge amongst the Amuesha of Central Peru*. London and Atlantic Highlands, NJ: Athlone Press, 1991.

Schultes, Richard Evans. *Vine of the Soul: Medicine Men, their Plants and Rituals in the Colombian Amazonia*. Oracle, AZ: Synergetic Press, 1992.

Slater, Candace. *Entangled Edens: Visions of the Amazon*. Berkeley: University of California Press, 2003.

———. *The Dance of the Dolphin: Transformation and Disenchantment in the Amazonian Imagination*. Chicago: University of Chicago Press, 1994.

Smith, Anthony. *Explorers of the Amazon*. Chicago: University Of Chicago Press, 1994.

Smith, Nigel J. H. *The Enchanted Amazon Rain Forest: Stories from a Vanishing World*. Gainesville: University of Florida Press, 1996.

———. *The Amazon River Forest: a Natural History of Plants, Animals, and People*. New York: Oxford University Press, 1999.

Souza, Marcio. *Breve história da Amazônia*. São Paulo: Marco Zero, 1994.

Sugobono, Nahuel, ed. *Mitos y leyendas del Amazonas*. Palma de Mallorca, España: J. J. de Olañeta, 1999.

Tagliani, Lino. *Mitología y cultura Huitoto*. Quito: ABYA-YALA, 1992.

Taussig, Michael. *Shamanism, Colonialism and the Wild Man: A Study in Terror and Healing*. Chicago: University of Chicago Press, 1991.

Uzendoski, Michael A. *The Napo Runa of Amazonian Ecuador*. Urbana: University of Illinois Press, 2005.

Whitehead, Neil L. *Dark Shamans: Kanaimà and the Poetics of Violent Death*. Durham, NC: Duke University Press, 2002.

Whitten, Norman E. *Sacha Runa: Ethnicity and Adaptation of Ecuadorian Jungle Quichua*. Urbana: University of Illinois Press, 1976.

Wilbert, Johannes. *Tobacco and Shamanism in South America*. London: Yale University Press, 1993.

Wilbert, Johannes, and Karin Simoneau, eds. *Folk Literature of the Gê Indians, Vol. II*. Los Angeles: University of California, UCLA Latin American Center for Publications, 1984.

APPENDIX: ANIMALS AND PLANTS OF AMAZONIAN CUISINE

Paca
(Agouti paca)

Tapir
(*Tapirus terrestris*)

Armadillo
(*Dasypus novemcinctus*)

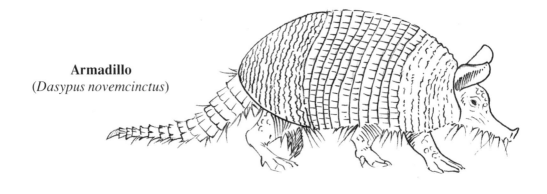

Appendix: Animals and Plants of Amazonian Cuisine

Peccary
(*Tayassu tajacu*)

Wooly Monkey
(*Lagothrix lagotricha*)

Tinamou
(*Crypturellus undulatus*)

Yellow Spotted River Turtle
(*Podocnemis unifilis*)

Pirarucu
(*Arapaima gigas*)

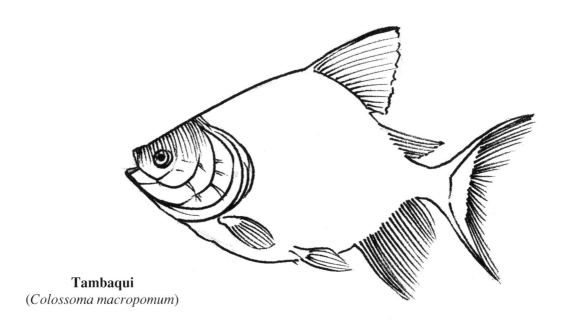

Tambaqui
(*Colossoma macropomum*)

Boquichico
(*Prochilodus nigricans*)

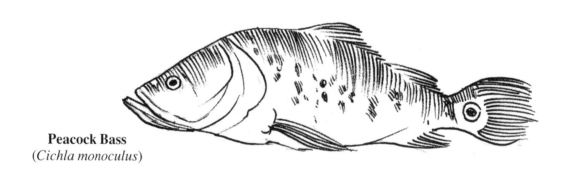

Peacock Bass
(*Cichla monoculus*)

Appendix: Animals and Plants of Amazonian Cuisine

Pijuayo Palm
(*Bactris gasipaes*)

Brazilian Nut Tree
(*Bertholletia excelsa*)

Assai Palm
(*Euterpe oleracea*)

Aguaje Palm
(*Mauritia flexuosa*)

Suri Palm Beetle Grubs
(*Rhynchophorus palmarum*)

Manioc Plant
(*Manihot esculenta*)

Guarana
(*Paullinia cupana*)

Appendix: Animals and Plants of Amazonian Cuisine

INDEX

Aguaje palm, *121*
Agouti paca, 113
Amasanga Warmi, 45–46
Anaconda
    The Girl and the
        Anaconda, 21–22
    Huayramama, 9–10
    Lupuna, 99–100
    Renacal, 93–94
    Yakumama, 13–14
Animal/plant protector. *See also* Forest
    protector
    Chullachaki, 43–44
    Epereji, 47–48
    Mapinguari, 39–40
    The Flute of the Chullachaki, 53–55
Aquatic abductor
    Mawaris, 30–31
Aquatic creatures. *See also* Anaconda;
    Dolphin
    María and the Dolphins, 19–20
    Yakumama, 13–14
Arapaima gigas, 117
Armadillo, *114*
Assai palm, *120*
Ayaymama, **97–98**

Bactris gasipaes, 119
Bertholletia excelsa, 119
Bird
    Ayaymama, 97–98
    Chicua, 101–102
    Matinta-Perera, 73–74
    Sachamama, 11–12
Boa
    Boa Plants, 95–96
    Juan Boa, 15–16

    Sachamama, 11–12
Boa Plants, 95–96
Boquichico, *118*
Brazilian nut tree, *119*

Caballococha, 87–88
Chicua, 101–102
Chullachaki, 43–44
Cichla monoculus, 118
The City of the Dolphins, 27–29
Colossoma macropomum, 117
Cowboy Quemdera, 85–86
Crypturellus undulatus, 116
Curupira, 41–42
Curupira's Son, 49–50

Dañero, 71–72
Dasypus novemcinctus, 114
Dolphin
    The City of the Dolphins, 27–29
    The Dolphin's Children, 34–35
    María and the Dolphins, 19–20
    Mawaris, 30–31
The Dolphin's Children, 34–35
Dream
    Curupira, 41–42
    The Dolphin's Children, 34–35
    Juan Boa, 15–16
    Lamparilla, 81–82
    María and the Dolphins, 19–20
    Renacal, 93–94

The Enchanted City, 91–92
Epereji, 47–48
Euterpe oleracea, 120
Evil spirits/ghosts
    Cowboy Quemdera, 85–86

Lamparilla, 81–82
Renacal, 93–94
Runamula, 83–84
The Spirits of the Stones, 66–67

The Flute of the Chullachaki, 53–55
Forest protector
    Curupira, 41–42
    Curupira's Son, 49–50
    The Hunter and the Curupira, 56–57
    Sachamama, 11–12

**A Gift from Yara, an Underwater Seducer,
    23–24**
The Girl and the Anaconda, 21–22
Greed
    Chullachaki, 43–44
    Curupira's Son, 49–50
    Epereji, 47–48
    The Flute of the Chullachaki, 53–55
    Moniyamena, 3–4
    Pact with the Devil, 69–70
    Renacal, 93–94
Guarana, *122*

Huayramama, 9–10
The Hunter and the Curupira, 56–57
Hunting
    Curupira, 41–42
    Curupira's Son, 49–50
    Epereji, 47–48
    The Flute of the Chullachaki, 53–55
    The Hunter and the Curupira, 56–57
    Mapinguari, 39–40
    Pumayuyu, 103–104
    Yanapuma, 58–59

Ill behavior, punishment for. *See also* Greed
    Caballococha, 87–88
    Cowboy Quemdera, 85–86
    Lamparilla, 81–82
    Runamula, 83–84
Immense trees and flowers. *See also* Rubber
    tree
    Amasanga Warmi, 45–46
    Lupuna, 99–100
    Moniyamena, 3–4
    Renacal, 93–94
    Vitória Régia, 5–6

Jaguar
    Lupuna, 99–100
    Pumayuyu, 103–104
    Yanapuma, 58–59
Juan Boa, 15–16

Kanaima, 63–65

Lagothrix lagotricha, 115
Lamparilla, 81–82
Lupuna, 99–100

Manibot esculenta, 121
Manioc plant, *121*
Mapinguari, 39–40
María and the Dolphins, 19–20
Matinta-Perera, 73–74
Mauritia flexuosa, 121
Mawaris, 30–31
Moniyamena, 3–4

Paca, *113*
Pact with the Devil, 69–70
Paullinia cupana, 122
Peacock bass, *118*
Peccary, *115*
Pijuayo palm, *119*
Pink dolphin. *See* Dolphin
Pirarucu, *117*
Podocnemis unifilis, 116
Prochilodus nigricans, 118
Pumayuyu, 103–104
Pusanga, 75–76

Renacal, 93–94
Rhynchophorus palmarum, 121
Rich cities in forest
    The Enchanted City, 91–92
Rubber tree. *See also* Immense trees and
    flowers
    Chullachaki, 43–44
    Pact with the Devil, 69–70
    Sachamama, 11–12
    Seringa, 51–52
Runamula, 83–84

Sacacas, 31
Sachamama (*Boa constrictor*), 10. *See also*
    Boa

Sachamama, 11–12
Seducer. *See also* Dolphin; Yakuruna; Yara
    Curupira's Son 49–50
    The Dolphin's Children, 34–35
    A Gift from Yara, an Underwater Seducer,
      23–24
    The Girl and the Anaconda, 21–22
    María and the Dolphins, 19–20
    Mawaris, 30–31
    Pusanga, 75–76
    Yakuruna, 25–26
    Yara, 32–33
Seringa, 51–52
Shaman
    Cowboy Quemdera, 85–86
    Dañero (dark shaman), 71–72
    The Dolphin's Children, 34–35
    Huayramama, 9–10
    Juan Boa, 15–16
    Kanaima (dark shaman), 63–64
    Lupuna, 99–100
    María and the Dolphins, 19–20
    Matinta-Perera, 73–74
    Mawaris, 30–31
    Pact with the Devil (dark shaman), 69–70
    Pumayuyu, 103–104
    Pusanga, 75–76
    Sachamama, 11–12
    The Spirits of the Stones (dark shaman), 66–67
    Yakuruna, 25–26
Snakes. *See* Anaconda; Boa
The Spirits of the Stones, 66–67
Suri palm beetle grubs, *121*

Tambaqui, *117*
Tapir, *114*
Tapirus terrestris, 114
Tayassu tajacu, 115
Tinamou, *116*
Tobacco smoke
    Chullachaki, 43–44

The City of the Dolphins, 27–29
Huayramama, 9–10
Lupuna, 99–100
Yakumama, 13–14
Yakuruna, 25–26
Transformations (humans into animals and
    vice versa)
    Amasanga Warmi, 45–46
    Ayaymama, 97–98
    Chicua, 101–102
    Curupira, 41–42
    Curupira's Son, 49–50
    Epereji, 47–48
    Juan Boa, 15–16
    Kanaima, 63–65
    María and the Dolphins, 19–20
    Matinta-Perera, 73–74
    Mawaris, 30–31
    Moniyamena, 3–4
    Pumayuyu, 103–104
    Runamula, 83–84
    Yara, 32–33

Vitória Régia, 5–6

Wooly monkey, *115*

Yachak. *See* Shaman
Yakumama (*Eunectes murinus*), 10. *See also*
    Anaconda
Yakumama, 13–14
Yakuruna, 25–26
Yanapuma, 58–59
Yara
    A Gift from Yara, an Underwater Seducer,
      23–24
    Yakumama, 13–14
    Yara, 32–33
Yara, 32–33
Yellow spotted river turtle, *116*

ABOUT THE AUTHOR

JUAN CARLOS GALEANO was born in the Amazon region of Colombia. He is the author of *Baraja Inicial* (poetry, 1986), *Pollen and Rifles* (1997) a book on the poetry of violence and *Amazonia* (poetry, 2003), whose poems received a Florida Individual Artist Fellowship in 2002. His poetry, inspired by Amazonian cosmologies and the modern world, has been published internationally and translated into French and English. It has been anthologized in a CD-ROM titled *Poesía Colombiana* (four centuries of Colombian poetry) produced by Casa Silva in Colombia, and in several anthologies in Latin America. Poems from *Amazonia* (2003) have been published in magazines  and journals such as *The Atlantic Monthly, Field, Ploughshares*, *TriQuarterly*, and *Antioch Review*. His poems and folktales have also appeared in college textbooks and in collections such as *Literary Amazonia* (2004), *The Poetry of Men's Lives: An International Anthology* (2004), and *The Encyclopedia of Religion and Nature* (2005). His research on Amazonian culture has appeared in his collection of folktales *Cuentos amazónicos* (2007) and in the film he codirected and coproduced, *The Trees Have a Mother* (2007). He also has published book-length translations of American poets in Latin America and translated Latin American poets for American journals. He teaches Latin American poetry at Florida State University.

ABOUT THE TRANSLATORS

REBECCA MORGAN teaches at the School of Teacher Education at Florida State University.

KENNETH WATSON, associate professor of English at the University of Southern Mississippi, is a specialist in nineteenth- and twentieth-century transatlantic literatures and cultures.